Life in the UK Test Questions & Study Guide 2025

Written By Michael Condon

The content contained within this book may not be reproduced, duplicated or transmitted without direct written permission from the author or the publisher. Under no circumstances will any blame or legal responsibility be held against the publisher, or author, for any damages, reparation, or monetary loss due to the information contained within this book. Either directly or indirectly. You are responsible for your own choices, actions, and results.

ISBN: 9798300343552

Chapter 1: Introduction

Welcome to the Life in the UK Test Study Guide! This comprehensive guide is designed to provide you with crucial information about life in the United Kingdom, including its history, values, institutions, and the rights and responsibilities of its residents. Whether you are preparing for the Life in the UK Test or seeking a deeper understanding of your new home, this guide will be a valuable resource.

Understanding the UK's history, values, and institutions is crucial not only for passing the Life in the UK Test but also for actively participating in and contributing to British society. Familiarizing yourself with the material in this guide will equip you with the knowledge needed to engage with your community, make informed decisions, and embrace your rights and responsibilities as a UK resident.

The Life in the UK Test is a requirement for individuals wishing to live in the UK permanently or apply for British citizenship. The test consists of 24 questions about key aspects of UK life, and you will have 45 minutes to complete it. This means you have just under 2 minutes per question, so manage your time wisely.

To pass, you need to answer at least 18 out of the 24 questions correctly, which is 75%. When you're ready to take the test, you can book online at www.lifeintheuktest.gov.uk. You will need a credit or debit card, an email address, and your ID. Tests are held at over 30 approved locations across the country, and you'll receive detailed instructions on where and when to attend. The test costs £50, and you can retake it as many times as needed until you pass.

We wish you all the best with your preparation!

Chapter 2: What is the UK?

With a rich history and a unique cultural heritage, the United Kingdom is a diverse and vibrant nation. It consists of four countries: England, Scotland, Wales, and Northern Ireland. The remainder of the island of Ireland is an independent nation known as the Republic of Ireland.

The full name of the country is the United Kingdom of Great Britain and Northern Ireland. In this book, you will encounter the terms Britain, Isles, or British to refer to people living in the UK. It's important to distinguish between Great Britain and the United Kingdom. Great Britain encompasses England, Scotland, and Wales, but excludes Northern Ireland. Note that Great Britain is a geographical term and does not represent a sovereign state or political entity.

Additionally, there are several islands closely associated with the United Kingdom but not part of it, such as the Channel Islands and the Isle of Man. These are known as "Crown dependencies" and have their own governments. The UK also maintains several overseas territories around the globe, including St Helena and the Falkland Islands, which are connected to the UK but not included within its borders.

The United Kingdom is governed by its Parliament in Westminster. Scotland, Wales, and Northern Ireland each have their own parliaments or assemblies with devolved powers in specific areas.

Note that "devolved powers" refers to the transfer of certain legislative and administrative powers from a central government to regional or local governments. In the context of the United Kingdom, this means that Scotland, Wales, and Northern Ireland have their own parliaments or assemblies that can make decisions and create laws in specific areas, such as education, health, and transportation, while the UK Parliament in Westminster retains authority over reserved matters like foreign policy and defense.

Revision Questions

Q1. Which of the following countries is not part of the United Kingdom?

A) England
B) Scotland
C) Wales
D) Republic of Ireland

Q2. What does the term "Great Britain" refer to?

A) A sovereign state including England, Scotland, and Wales
B) The entire United Kingdom including Northern Ireland
C) A geographical term for the island comprising England, Scotland, and Wales
D) A political entity that includes Northern Ireland

Q3. Which term is used to describe the islands that are associated with but not part of the United Kingdom, such as the Channel Islands and the Isle of Man?

A) British Overseas Territories
B) Crown Dependencies
C) Independent States
D) Autonomous Regions

Q4. What is the official name of the United Kingdom?

A) The United Kingdom of Great Britain and Ireland
B) The United Kingdom of Great Britain and Northern Ireland
C) The United Kingdom of England and Wales
D) The United Kingdom of Scotland and Northern Ireland

Q5. Where is the Parliament that governs the United Kingdom located?

A) Edinburgh
B) Cardiff
C) Belfast
D) Westminster

Answers

Q1. Which of the following countries is not part of the United Kingdom?

Answer: D – Republic of Ireland

Q2. What does the term "Great Britain" refer to?

Answer: C – A geographical term for the island comprising England, Scotland, and Wales

Q3. Which term is used to describe the islands that are associated with but not part of the United Kingdom, such as the Channel Islands and the Isle of Man?

Answer: B – Crown Dependencies

Q4. What is the official name of the United Kingdom?

Answer: B – The United Kingdom of Great Britain and Northern Ireland

Q5. Where is the Parliament that governs the United Kingdom located?

Answer: D – Westminster

Chapter 3: A Long & Inspiring History

Early Britain

Hunter-gatherers were the first inhabitants of Britain during the Stone Age. For much of this period, Britain was connected to mainland Europe by a land bridge, allowing people to travel back and forth on foot. It was only about 10,000 years ago that the English Channel formed, permanently separating Britain from the continent.

Around 6,000 years ago, the first farmers arrived in Britain, believed to have come from southeast Europe. They built houses, tombs, and monuments across the land. Stonehenge in Wiltshire, England, is a famous example of their construction and likely served as a special site for seasonal ceremonies. Another notable site is Skara Brae on Orkney, off the northeastern coast of Scotland. This well-preserved prehistoric village has given archaeologists valuable insights into life at the end of the Stone Age.

Approximately 2,000 years later, around 4,000 years ago, the Bronze Age began with the discovery of bronze. This period saw skilled metalworkers creating intricate ornaments, tools, and weapons from bronze and gold. People lived in circular houses and buried their dead in round barrows.

The Bronze Age was succeeded by the Iron Age, during which iron began to be used for tools and weapons. Settlements grew larger and were often fortified with hill forts, such as Maiden Castle in Dorset, England. Iron Age society was advanced, with the production of coins bearing the names of kings. Most people were farmers, craftsmen, or warriors, and spoke a Celtic language. Similar Celtic languages were used across Europe during this time, and some related languages are still spoken in parts of Ireland, Scotland, and Wales today.

The Romans

In 55 BC, Julius Caesar attempted to invade Britain but failed. For nearly a century, Britain stayed independent from the Roman Empire. It wasn't until AD 43 that Emperor Claudius launched another invasion. Despite strong resistance from British tribes, the Romans managed to conquer almost all of Britain. One of the most notable resistors was Boudicca, queen of the Iceni tribe in eastern England. Her struggle is remembered today with a statue on Westminster Bridge in London, near the Houses of Parliament.

The Romans ruled Britain for about 400 years. During their rule, they built public buildings and roads, introduced new plants and animals, and set up a legal system. The first Christian communities in Britain appeared during the 3rd and 4th centuries AD.

However, parts of what is now Scotland were never conquered by the Romans. To protect against the Picts, the ancestors of the Scottish people, Emperor Hadrian built a large wall across northern England. Known as Hadrian's Wall, it included several forts. Today, parts of this ancient wall, including the forts at Housesteads and Vindolanda, are still visible and attract many visitors. Hadrian's Wall is also recognised as a UNESCO World Heritage Site for its historical importance.

The Anglo-Saxons

In AD 410, the Roman army withdrew from Britain to defend other parts of the Roman Empire and never returned. This departure allowed tribes from northern Europe, including the Jutes, Angles, and Saxons, to invade Britain. The languages these tribes spoke laid the groundwork for modern English. Despite resistance, by around AD 600, Anglo-Saxon kingdoms had been established in Britain, primarily in what is now England. One notable burial site from this period is Sutton Hoo in Suffolk, where a king's treasure and armor were interred in a ship and covered with a mound of earth. However, large areas of western Britain, including much of Wales and Scotland, remained outside Anglo-Saxon control.

Initially, the Anglo-Saxons were not Christians. However, during this time, missionaries arrived to spread Christianity. Irish missionaries, such as St Patrick, who later became the patron saint of Ireland, and St Columba, who founded a monastery on the island of Iona off the Scottish coast, played key roles in the north. In the south, St Augustine led missionaries from Rome, spreading Christianity and becoming the first Archbishop of Canterbury.

The Vikings

The Vikings, originating from Denmark and Norway, first arrived in Britain in AD 789. Their initial incursions involved raiding coastal towns, stealing goods, and capturing slaves. They also established their own settlements in eastern England and Scotland.

King Alfred the Great successfully united the Anglo-Saxon kingdoms of England and defeated the Vikings. Despite this, many Viking invaders remained, particularly in the Danelaw—a region in the east and north of England known for its Viking-influenced place names like Grimsby and Scunthorpe. There, Vikings integrated with local communities, and some even converted to Christianity.

The Anglo-Saxon kings continued to rule what is now England, with a brief interruption when Danish kings, including Cnut (or Canute), held power. In the north, the threat of Viking raids led to the unification of the people under Kenneth MacAlpin, marking the beginning of the term "Scotland" to describe the region.

The Norman Conquest

In 1066, William, Duke of Normandy (a region in what is now northern France), led an invasion that defeated Harold, the Saxon king of England, at the Battle of Hastings, fought near Hastings in East Sussex. Harold was killed in the battle, and William claimed the English throne, earning the title William the Conqueror. To commemorate the battle, the Bayeux Tapestry was created, and it remains on display in France today.

The Norman Conquest marked the last successful foreign invasion of England and brought significant changes to the country's government and social structures. The language of the new ruling class, Norman French, had a lasting impact on the development of the English language. Although the Normans initially conquered Wales, the Welsh gradually regained much of their territory. On the border between England and Scotland, the Normans and Scots clashed, with the Normans capturing some land but opting not to invade further into Scotland.

Following his victory and ascension to the English throne, William ordered a detailed survey of towns, villages, landowners, and livestock across England. This survey was recorded in the Domesday Book, a valuable historical document that offers a detailed snapshot of English society after the Norman Conquest.

The Normans introduced feudalism, a system where the king granted land to lords in return for military service. These lords were required to provide soldiers for the army, while most peasants worked the land as serfs and were not allowed to leave. Some peasants had small plots of land for growing their own food.

A similar feudal system developed in southern Scotland, while land in northern Scotland and Ireland was controlled by prominent families or clans.

Revision Questions

Q1. Who were the first inhabitants of Britain during the Stone Age?

A) Romans
B) Anglo-Saxons
C) Vikings
D) Hunter-gatherers

Q2. How long ago did the English Channel form, separating Britain from the mainland?

A) 4,000 years
B) 6,000 years
C) 8,000 years
D) 10,000 years

Q3. Which site is known for its famous stone monument built around 6,000 years ago?

A) Skara Brae
B) Maiden Castle
C) Hadrian's Wall
D) Stonehenge

Q4. What was the main material used during the Bronze Age to create tools and weapons?

A) Stone
B) Iron
C) Bronze
D) Gold

Q5. During which age did people live in circular houses and bury their dead in round barrows?

A) Iron Age
B) Stone Age
C) Bronze Age
D) Roman Era

Q6. Who attempted to invade Britain in 55 BC but was unsuccessful?

A) Emperor Claudius
B) Julius Caesar
C) Boudicca
D) William the Conqueror

Q7. What was the name of the wall built by Emperor Hadrian to protect against the Picts?

A) Antonine Wall
B) Roman Wall
C) Hadrian's Wall
D) London Wall

Q8. Which group of tribes invaded Britain after the Roman army withdrew in AD 410?

A) Celts
B) Normans
C) Anglo-Saxons
D) Danes

Q9. Who led the successful invasion of Britain in 1066, defeating King Harold at the Battle of Hastings?

A) William the Conqueror
B) Julius Caesar
C) King Alfred
D) Cnut

Q10. What document, ordered by William the Conqueror, provides a detailed record of English society after the Norman Conquest?

A) The Magna Carta
B) The Bayeux Tapestry
C) The Domesday Book
D) The Doomsday Survey

Answers

Q1. Who were the first inhabitants of Britain during the Stone Age?
Answer: D – Hunter-gatherers

Q2. How long ago did the English Channel form, separating Britain from the mainland?
Answer: D – 10,000 years

Q3. Which site is known for its famous stone monument built around 6,000 years ago?
Answer: D – Stonehenge
Note: Stonehenge in Wiltshire is a well-known prehistoric monument built by the first farmers in Britain.

Q4. What was the main material used during the Bronze Age to create tools and weapons?
Answer: C – Bronze

Q5. During which age did people live in circular houses and bury their dead in round barrows?
Answer: C – Bronze Age

Q6. Who attempted to invade Britain in 55 BC but was unsuccessful?
Answer: B – Julius Caesar

Q7. What was the name of the wall built by Emperor Hadrian to protect against the Picts?
Answer C – Hadrian's Wall

Q8. Which group of tribes invaded Britain after the Roman army withdrew in AD 410?
Answer: C – Anglo-Saxons

Q9. Who led the successful invasion of Britain in 1066, defeating King Harold at the Battle of Hastings?
Answer: A – William the Conqueror

Q10. What document, ordered by William the Conqueror, provides a detailed record of English society after the Norman Conquest?
Answer: C – The Domesday Book
Note: The Domesday Book was a comprehensive survey ordered by William the Conqueror to document towns, landowners, and resources in England.

The Middle Ages

War At Home & Abroad

The period between the Norman Conquest and 1485 is referred to as the Middle Ages or Medieval period. This era was characterised by almost constant conflict as English kings fought to control Wales, Scotland, and Ireland.

In Wales, English control was solidified through the Statute of Rhuddlan in 1284, which annexed the territory. To enforce their rule, the English built imposing castles like Conwy and Caernarfon. By the mid-15th century, English laws and the English language had been firmly established, and the last Welsh uprisings were suppressed.

In Scotland, however, English attempts to conquer the region were largely unsuccessful. Scotland remained independent, with a significant victory for the Scots occurring in 1314 at the Battle of Bannockburn, where Robert the Bruce defeated the English forces.

Ireland, meanwhile, began the Middle Ages as an independent country. The English first arrived to support an Irish king but eventually established their own settlements. By 1200, the English had asserted control over an area around Dublin known as the Pale, though their authority was recognised by only some Irish lords.

English kings also engaged in overseas conflicts during the Middle Ages. Many knights participated in the Crusades, a series of military campaigns aimed at capturing the Holy Land. Additionally, the English fought the Hundred Years' War against France, a protracted conflict lasting 116 years. A notable victory occurred at the Battle of Agincourt in 1415, where King Henry V led an outnumbered English army to triumph over the French. The English eventually withdrew from France in the 1450s.

The Black Death

In 1348, the Black Death, a disease likely caused by the bubonic plague, arrived in Britain, killing a third of the population in England, Scotland, and Wales. It was one of the deadliest disasters in Britain's history. After the Black Death, the reduced population led to a major decrease in cereal crop production and peasants demanded higher wages due to labour shortages. The emergence of new social classes, including large landowners (later known as the gentry), and migration from the countryside to towns led to the growth of a strong middle class.

In Ireland, the Black Death hit the Pale hard, causing the English-controlled area to shrink temporarily.

Legal & Political Changes

During the Middle Ages, Parliament began to evolve into its current form, originating from the king's council of advisers that included prominent noblemen and Church leaders. Until 1215, the king wielded almost absolute power. However, that year marked a turning point when King John was compelled to accept the Magna Carta, a charter of rights that asserted the principle that even the king is subject to the law. This landmark document mandated the king to consult his nobles in decision-making and placed limits on his authority to levy taxes and enact laws.

In England, Parliaments were convened primarily to consult with nobles, especially when the king needed to raise funds. As time progressed, the number of Parliament attendees grew, leading to the establishment of two separate Houses: the House of Lords, which comprised nobles, significant landowners, and bishops, and the House of Commons, made up of knights, smaller landowners, and wealthy citizens from towns and cities. However, only a small fraction of the population had the right to vote for Commons representatives.

In Scotland, a similar parliamentary structure emerged, consisting of three Estates: the Lords, the Commons, and the Clergy.

The Middle Ages also saw the development of the legal system, with the principle of judicial independence taking root. In England, judges established "common law" based on precedent and tradition, while in Scotland, laws were codified, meaning they were formally documented.

The Wars of the Roses

In 1455, England was plunged into a civil war known as the Wars of the Roses, which was fought between two rival families: the House of Lancaster and the House of York. The conflict earned its name from the emblems of the opposing sides: the red rose of Lancaster and the white rose of York.

The war ended in 1485 with the Battle of Bosworth Field, where King Richard III of the House of York was defeated. Henry Tudor, leader of the House of Lancaster, emerged victorious and became King Henry VII. To solidify peace, Henry married Elizabeth of York, Richard III's niece. This marriage united the two warring houses, and Henry became the first monarch of the House of Tudor, whose emblem combined a red rose and a white rose, symbolizing the merger of the two families.

Revision Questions

Q1. What year did the Black Death arrive in Britain?

A) 2000
B) 1348
C) 1455
D) 2019

Q2. What was a major consequence of the Black Death on the English economy?

A) Increase in crop production
B) Decrease in labor wages
C) Increase in labor wages
D) Expansion of English territory

Q3. Which English king was forced to sign the Magna Carta in 1215?

A) Henry III
B) Richard the Lionheart
C) John
D) Edward I

Q4. How did the Magna Carta affect the power of the English king?

A) It gave the king more control over taxes
B) It allowed the king to ignore nobles
C) It established that the king was also subject to the law
D) It eliminated the need for a Parliament

Q5. What significant battle ended the Wars of the Roses?

A) Battle of Bannockburn
B) Battle of Hastings
C) Battle of Agincourt
D) Battle of Bosworth Field

Q6. Which two houses were involved in the Wars of the Roses?

A) House of Lancaster and House of York
B) House of Tudor and House of Stuart
C) House of Plantagenet and House of Tudor
D) House of York and House of Stuart

Q7. Who became king of England after the Battle of Bosworth Field?

A) Richard III
B) Edward IV
C) Henry VII
D) Henry VIII

Q8. How did Henry VII unite the Houses of Lancaster and York?

A) By creating a new royal emblem
B) By marrying Elizabeth of York
C) By conquering Scotland
D) By signing the Magna Carta

Q9. What was the impact of the Crusades on English knights?

A) They gained control of Ireland
B) They improved relations with Scotland
C) They participated in military campaigns to capture the Holy Land
D) They were involved in the Wars of the Roses

Answers

Q1. What year did the Black Death arrive in Britain?
Answer: B – 1348

Q2. What was a major consequence of the Black Death on the English economy?
Answer: C – Increase in labor wages
Note: Due to the labor shortage caused by the Black Death, peasants demanded higher wages, which led to significant economic changes.

Q3. Which English king was forced to sign the Magna Carta in 1215?
Answer: C – John
Note: King John was compelled to sign the Magna Carta, which limited his powers and set important legal precedents.

Q4. How did the Magna Carta affect the power of the English king?
Answer: C – It established that the king was also subject to the law
Note: The Magna Carta established the principle that even the king had to follow the law and involved nobles in decision-making.

Q5. What significant battle ended the Wars of the Roses?
Answer: D – Battle of Bosworth Field
Note: The Battle of Bosworth Field in 1485 marked the end of the Wars of the Roses and the rise of the Tudor dynasty.

Q6. Which two houses were involved in the Wars of the Roses?
Answer: A – House of Lancaster and House of York

Q7. Who became king of England after the Battle of Bosworth Field?
Answer: King Henry VII
Note: Henry Tudor, who became King Henry VII, won the Battle of Bosworth Field and started the Tudor dynasty.

Q8. How did Henry VII unite the Houses of Lancaster and York?
Answer: B – By marrying Elizabeth of York

Q9. What was the impact of the Crusades on English knights?
Answer: C – They participated in military campaigns to capture the Holy Land

The Tudors and Stuarts

After his victory in the Wars of the Roses, Henry VII worked to secure his reign by centralizing England's administration and limiting the power of the nobility. He was careful with finances, focusing on strengthening the monarchy's resources. His son, Henry VIII, continued this focus on centralizing power.

Henry VIII is most famous for his dramatic break from the Roman Catholic Church. He wanted to annul his marriage to Catherine of Aragon to marry Anne Boleyn. When the Pope refused to grant the annulment, Henry created the Church of England and declared himself its head, effectively severing ties with Rome. Henry VIII went on to marry six times, including Anne Boleyn, Jane Seymour, Anne of Cleves, Catherine Howard, and Catherine Parr.

The Six Wives of Henry VIII

1. Catherine of Aragon – A Spanish princess, Catherine was Henry's first wife. They had several children, but only their daughter Mary survived. When Catherine could no longer bear children, Henry sought a divorce, hoping a new wife would give him a male heir.

2. Anne Boleyn – An English noblewoman, Anne was Henry's second wife and the mother of Elizabeth. Her unpopularity and accusations of infidelity led to her execution at the Tower of London.

3. Jane Seymour – Henry's third wife, Jane gave him the long-desired male heir, Edward. Unfortunately, she died shortly after childbirth.

4. Anne of Cleves – A German princess, Anne was Henry's fourth wife. Their marriage was politically motivated but ended in divorce soon after.

5. Catherine Howard – A cousin of Anne Boleyn, Catherine was Henry's fifth wife. She was accused of infidelity and was executed.

6. Catherine Parr – Henry's sixth and final wife, Catherine was a widow who married Henry late in his life. She survived him and later married again but died shortly after.

To divorce Catherine of Aragon, Henry VIII needed the Pope's approval. When the Pope refused, Henry broke away from the Roman Catholic Church and established the Church of England, giving himself the authority to appoint bishops and control religious practices. This move was part of the broader Reformation across Europe, where many rejected the Pope's authority and formed their own churches. In England, Wales, and Scotland, Protestantism began to take hold, but efforts to impose it in Ireland led to conflict and unrest.

During Henry's reign, Wales was formally integrated with England through the Act for the Government of Wales, and the Welsh legal system was reformed. Henry was succeeded by his son, Edward VI, who was a strong Protestant. Edward's reign saw the creation of the Book of Common Prayer for use in the Church of England. Edward died young, at just 15, and was followed by his half-sister Mary, a committed Catholic who persecuted Protestants. After Mary's death, her half-sister Elizabeth, the daughter of Henry and Anne Boleyn, became queen.

Queen Elizabeth I

Queen Elizabeth I, a Protestant, reinstated the Church of England as the country's official religion. Under her rule, attendance at local churches and adherence to certain religious laws were required, but she did not scrutinise individuals' personal beliefs. Elizabeth skilfully navigated between Catholic and more radical Protestant views, avoiding major religious conflicts within England. Her reputation as a respected monarch was solidified after the English navy's triumph over the Spanish Armada in 1588, a fleet sent by Spain to invade England and restore Catholicism.

The Reformation in Scotland and Mary, Queen of Scots

In 1560, Scotland experienced a significant shift towards Protestantism. The largely Protestant Scottish Parliament removed the Pope's authority from Scotland, making Roman Catholic services illegal. Instead, a Protestant Church of Scotland was formed with its own independent leadership, though it was not established as a state church like in England.

Mary Stuart, also known as Mary, Queen of Scots, was a Catholic who became queen at just a week old following her father's death. She spent much of her childhood in France and faced a turbulent return to Scotland, where she was caught in political conflicts. After her husband's murder, Mary, who was suspected of involvement, fled to England and abdicated the Scottish throne in favor of her Protestant son, James VI. Although Mary was Elizabeth I's cousin and sought her support, Elizabeth suspected Mary of plotting to claim the English throne and kept her imprisoned for 20 years. Mary was ultimately executed after being accused of conspiring against Elizabeth.

Exploration, Poetry and Drama

The Elizabethan era was a time of growing national pride for England. English explorers sought new trade routes and expanded British commerce, reaching into Spanish colonies in the Americas. Sir Francis Drake, a key figure in England's naval history, played a major role in defeating the Spanish Armada and became the first Englishman to sail around the world in his ship, the Golden Hind. During Queen Elizabeth I's reign, English settlers established the first colonies along the eastern coast of America. These colonies grew significantly in the following century, particularly as people who disagreed with the religious views of the subsequent kings migrated there.

The Elizabethan era was also a golden age for literature, especially for the works of William Shakespeare, whose poetry and plays were widely celebrated.

William Shakespeare (1564–1616)

William Shakespeare, the celebrated English playwright and actor, was born in Stratford-upon-Avon, England. He authored a vast array of works, including iconic plays such as *A Midsummer Night's Dream*, *Hamlet*, *Macbeth*, and *Romeo and Juliet*.

He is widely regarded as the greatest playwright of all time, and his works remain influential and widely performed across the globe. Today, the Globe Theatre in

London stands as a modern reconstruction of the original venue where his plays were first staged.

Shakespeare was pioneering in his depiction of everyday English people and his dramatisation of historical events. His influence on the English language was profound; he coined many words and phrases that are still widely used today. Notable lines from his plays and poems continue to be quoted frequently, reflecting his lasting impact.

"Once more unto the breach" (Henry V),

"To be or not to be" (Hamlet),

"A rose by any other name" (Romeo and Juliet),

"All the world's a stage" (As You Like It), and

"The darling buds of May" (Sonnet 18 – Shall I Compare Thee to a Summer's Day?).

King James Bible

When Elizabeth I died in 1603, her cousin James VI of Scotland succeeded her as King James I of England, Wales, and Ireland. Despite this, Scotland remained an independent country under his reign. Among his significant achievements was commissioning the translation of the Bible into English, which led to the creation of the "King James Version" or "Authorised Version." Although not the first English translation, it continues to be widely used in many Protestant churches today.

Ireland

During the Middle Ages, Ireland was mainly a Catholic country. The English slowly extended their control across the island, including the Pale, and established their authority over the entire country. Henry VIII even declared himself "King of Ireland." English laws were implemented, and local leaders were expected to adhere to the orders of the Lord Lieutenants in Dublin.

Under Elizabeth I and James I, opposition to English Protestant rule in Ireland led to several rebellions. In response, the English government encouraged Scottish and English Protestants to settle in Ulster, the northern province, displacing Catholic landholders. These settlements, known as plantations, included many settlers from southwest Scotland and land allocated to companies based in London. James I later initiated similar plantations in other parts of Ireland, which had significant long-term impacts on the history of England, Scotland, and Ireland.

The Rise of Parliament

Elizabeth I was highly skilled at managing Parliament, adeptly balancing her own views with those of the increasingly Protestant House of Commons and the House of Lords.

In contrast, her successors, James I and his son Charles I, struggled with political maneuvering. Both believed in the Divine Right of Kings, the idea that monarchs were appointed by God and could rule without needing Parliament's consent. When Charles I ascended the thrones of England, Wales, Ireland, and Scotland, he tried to govern based on this principle. When Parliament opposed his religious and foreign policies, he attempted to rule without it, managing to raise funds independently for 11 years. However, escalating issues in Scotland eventually forced him to summon Parliament again.

The Start of the English Civil War

Charles I sought to make the Church of England more ceremonial and introduced a revised Prayer Book. When he attempted to enforce these changes on the Presbyterian Church in Scotland, it caused widespread unrest and led to the formation of a Scottish army. To respond, Charles needed funds, prompting him to recall Parliament in 1640. However, many Parliament members were Puritans who opposed his religious reforms, and they refused to provide the requested funds, escalating tensions between the king and Parliament.

Simultaneously, a rebellion erupted in Ireland as Roman Catholics feared the rising influence of the Puritans. Parliament demanded control over the English army, which would shift power away from the king. In response, Charles I entered the House of Commons to arrest five parliamentary leaders, who had been warned and were absent. This confrontation ignited the Civil War in 1642, dividing the country between supporters of the king (the Cavaliers) and supporters of Parliament (the Roundheads).

Oliver Cromwell & the English Republic

After the king's defeat at the Battles of Marston Moor and Naseby, it became clear by 1646 that Parliament had won the English Civil War. Charles I was captured by the parliamentary forces but refused to negotiate, leading to his execution in 1649. England then declared itself a republic known as the Commonwealth, abolishing the monarchy.

The country's future governance was uncertain for a time. The army, led by General Oliver Cromwell, took charge and was sent to Ireland to address the ongoing revolt and assert the authority of the English Parliament. Cromwell's harsh methods were controversial and he remains a contentious figure in Ireland today.

In Scotland, Charles I's supporters refused to accept his execution and declared his son, Charles II, as king. Charles II led a Scottish army into England but was defeated by Cromwell at the Battles of Dunbar and Worcester. Charles II escaped to Europe, leaving Parliament in control of England, Scotland, and Wales.

After his successful campaigns in Ireland and against Charles II, Cromwell was appointed Lord Protector of the new republic. He ruled until his death in 1658, after which his son Richard briefly became Lord Protector. However, Richard struggled to manage the army and government, leading many to call for the restoration of the monarchy to provide stability.

The Restoration

In May 1660, Parliament invited Charles II to end his exile in the Netherlands and return as the King of England, Wales, Scotland, and Ireland. Charles II recognised that he needed to cooperate with Parliament and reach agreements on various matters. During his reign, Parliament supported his policies and reaffirmed the

Church of England as the state church, excluding both Roman Catholics and Puritans from positions of power.

A major event during Charles II's reign was the outbreak of the plague in London in 1665, which led to thousands of deaths, particularly among the poor. The following year, the Great Fire of London swept through the city, destroying much of it, including St. Paul's Cathedral. The city was rebuilt, and a new St. Paul's Cathedral was designed by the renowned architect Sir Christopher Wren. These calamities and their aftermath were famously recorded in Samuel Pepys's diary, which remains a valuable historical source.

Additionally, in 1679, the Habeas Corpus Act was enacted under Charles II, ensuring that no one could be imprisoned unlawfully and that every prisoner had the right to a court hearing. Charles II also had a keen interest in science and played a role in founding the Royal Society, which promotes scientific knowledge. This society, the oldest scientific institution in the world, included notable members such as Sir Edmund Halley, known for predicting the return of Halley's Comet, and Sir Isaac Newton.

Isaac Newton (1643–1727)

Isaac Newton, born in Lincolnshire in eastern England, developed a deep interest in science during his time at Cambridge University. He became a pivotal figure in the field, and his most famous work, *Philosophiæ Naturalis Principia Mathematica* (Mathematical Principles of Natural Philosophy), established the universal law of gravitation. Newton also made the groundbreaking discovery that white light is made up of the colours of the rainbow. His contributions have had a lasting impact on modern science.

A Catholic King

Charles II, who had no legitimate heirs, passed away in 1685. He was succeeded by his brother, James II, who became King James II of England, Wales, and Ireland, and James VII of Scotland. A Roman Catholic, James II favored Catholics, allowing them to hold positions as army officers despite an Act of Parliament prohibiting this. He also clashed with Parliament, arresting some Anglican bishops, which fueled fears that he intended to reestablish Catholicism in England. Although James II's two daughters were Protestant, making a Protestant succession seem likely, the birth of a son raised concerns that the future monarch might be Catholic after all.

The Glorious Revolution

In 1688, William of Orange, the Protestant ruler of the Netherlands and husband of James II's eldest daughter, Mary, was invited by prominent Protestants in England to invade and claim the throne. James II fled to France, and William and Mary began their joint rule as William III and Mary II. This event, known as the "Glorious Revolution," marked the end of absolute monarchy and established the principle that the king could not govern without Parliament's consent.

Despite this, James II sought to reclaim his throne and launched an invasion of Ireland with French support. William defeated James at the Battle of the Boyne in 1690, reasserting control over Ireland. Following this victory, restrictions were imposed on the Roman Catholic Church in Ireland, and Catholics were barred from participating in government.

Support for James persisted in Scotland, leading to an attempted rebellion that was quickly crushed at the Battle of Killiecrankie. All Scottish clans were required to swear allegiance to William, and the MacDonalds of Glencoe, who were late in taking the oath, were massacred, fostering resentment towards the new regime. James's supporters, known as Jacobites, continued to advocate for his claim to the throne.

Revision Questions

Q1. What was the primary reason for the Glorious Revolution of 1688?

A) To end the English Civil War
B) To establish William III and Mary II as rulers
C) To support James II's absolute monarchy
D) To address the conflict in Ireland

Q2. What action did James II take that led to widespread concern among English Protestants?

A) He strengthened the Church of England
B) He appointed Roman Catholics to high positions and ignored Parliament
C) He increased taxes significantly
D) He withdrew from Parliament

Q3. Which battle in 1690 was decisive in reaffirming William III's control over Ireland?

A) The Battle of Killiecrankie
B) The Battle of Marston Moor
C) The Battle of the Boyne
D) The Battle of Naseby

Q4. How did the Glorious Revolution affect the relationship between the monarchy and Parliament?

A) It strengthened the monarchy's absolute power
B) It ended the monarchy entirely
C) It established a constitutional monarchy with Parliament's consent
D) It led to frequent changes in monarchs

Q5. What was the fate of James II's supporters in Scotland after his defeat?

A) They were given government positions
B) They formed a new political party
C) They were required to accept William as king, with some facing severe consequences
D) They moved to Ireland

Q6. What was the main reason for James II's invasion of Ireland?

A) To reclaim the English throne
B) To seek alliances with French troops
C) To gain control over trade routes
D) To establish a new monarchy

Q7. What was the impact of the Battle of Killiecrankie on James II's supporters in Scotland?

A) It led to their complete victory
B) It was a decisive defeat for James II's forces
C) It resulted in a peace treaty
D) It ended their support for James II

Q8. What were the Jacobites known for in the aftermath of the Glorious Revolution?

A) Supporting William III
B) Supporting the Union of England and Scotland
C) Supporting James II as the rightful king
D) Establishing a new form of government

Q9. True or false? One of the major consequences for Irish Catholics after the Battle of the Boyne was exclusion from government participation.

Q10. How did William of Orange become the king of England, Wales, Scotland, and Ireland?

A) Through a military coup
B) By being invited by important Protestants and marrying James II's daughter
C) By inheriting the throne
D) Through a peaceful negotiation with James II

Answers

Q1. What was the primary reason for the Glorious Revolution of 1688?

Answer: B – To establish William III and Mary II as rulers

Note: The Glorious Revolution established William III and Mary II as rulers of England, Wales, and Ireland, ending the threat of absolute monarchy.

Q2. What action did James II take that led to widespread concern among English Protestants?

Answer: B – He appointed Roman Catholics to high positions and ignored Parliament

Q3. Which battle in 1690 was decisive in reaffirming William III's control over Ireland?

Answer: C – The Battle of the Boyne

Q4. How did the Glorious Revolution affect the relationship between the monarchy and Parliament?

Answer: C – It established a constitutional monarchy with Parliament's consent

Note: This change effectively limited the monarch's power in favor of the Parliament's authority.

Q5. What was the fate of James II's supporters in Scotland after his defeat?

Answer: C – They were required to accept William as king, with some facing severe consequences

Q6. What was the main reason for James II's invasion of Ireland?

Answer: A – To reclaim the English throne
Note: James II invaded Ireland to reclaim the English throne, seeking support from the French army.

Q7. What was the impact of the Battle of Killiecrankie on James II's supporters in Scotland?

Answer: B – It was a decisive defeat for James II's forces

Note: This decisive defeat effectively ended their rebellion.

Q8. What were the Jacobites known for in the aftermath of the Glorious Revolution?

Answer: C – Supporting James II as the rightful king

Note: Jacobites were known for supporting James II as the rightful king and continuing to believe in his claim to the throne.

Q9. True or false? One of the major consequences for Irish Catholics after the Battle of the Boyne was exclusion from government participation.

Answer: True – They were excluded from government participation

Q10. How did William of Orange become the king of England, Wales, Scotland, and Ireland?

Answer: B – By being invited by important Protestants and marrying James II's daughter

A Global Power

Constitutional Monarchy: The Bill of Rights

At the coronation of William III and Mary II, a Declaration of Rights was proclaimed, which set forth that the monarch could no longer levy taxes or administer justice without Parliament's consent. This declaration marked a significant shift in the balance of power between the monarchy and Parliament. The Bill of Rights, enacted in 1689, reinforced the rights of Parliament and imposed limits on the monarch's authority. It required the monarch to be Protestant and mandated that a new Parliament be elected at least every three years. Additionally, the monarch had to seek Parliament's approval to renew funding for the army and navy annually.

These developments underscored the need for ministers capable of securing a majority in both the House of Commons and the House of Lords. Consequently, two major political factions emerged in Parliament: the Whigs and the Tories, signifying the beginning of party politics.

Whigs and Tories

The term "Whigs" originated in Scotland and was first used to describe Scottish Presbyterian rebels who opposed King Charles I's policies in the 1640s. It is thought to have come from the Scottish Gaelic word "whiggam," meaning "drive" or "horse driver," and was initially used as a derogatory term for these rebels.

The name "Tory," on the other hand, has Irish roots and emerged during the Exclusion Crisis in the late 1670s. It is believed to be derived from the Irish word "tóraidhe," meaning "outlaw" or "pursuer." Supporters of King Charles II's brother, James, Duke of York, who opposed excluding James from the throne due to his Catholic faith, were labeled "Tories."

During this period, the emergence of a free press began, with newspapers permitted to operate without government licensing starting in 1695.

The laws enacted following the Glorious Revolution established a "constitutional monarchy," where the monarch's authority was constrained by parliamentary agreement. Despite these advancements, voting rights remained restricted; only property-owning men were eligible to vote, while women had no voting rights. Additionally, some constituencies were dominated by wealthy families, and others had very few voters, known as "rotten boroughs."

A Growing Population

In the 17th and 18th centuries, there was considerable migration to and from Britain and Ireland. Many people left for new colonies in America and other regions, while others moved to Britain. In 1656, the first Jewish settlers since the Middle Ages arrived in London. Additionally, between 1680 and 1720, French Protestants known as the Huguenots came to Britain as refugees, fleeing religious persecution. Many of these Huguenots were skilled and educated in fields such as science, banking, weaving, and various crafts.

The Act of Treaty or Union in Scotland

In 1707, the Act of Union was enacted, establishing the Kingdom of Great Britain. This was prompted by the death of Queen Anne, who had no surviving heirs, leading to concerns about the future succession in England, Wales, Ireland, and Scotland. Although Scotland lost its status as an independent nation, it retained its own legal and educational systems, as well as the Presbyterian Church. The Act also unified the parliaments of England and Scotland into a single parliament.

The Prime Minister

In 1714, following the death of Queen Anne, Parliament selected George I, a German prince and the nearest Protestant relative of Anne, to become the new king of England, Wales, Scotland, and Ireland. Although the Scottish Jacobites attempted to install James II's son on the throne, their efforts were swiftly quelled. George I, who was not fluent in English, depended greatly on his ministers, leading to the emergence of the Prime Minister as the most prominent figure in Parliament. Sir Robert Walpole, who served from 1721 to 1742, was the first person to hold this title.

The Rebellion of the Clans

In 1745, Charles Edward Stuart, also known as Bonnie Prince Charlie and the grandson of James II, attempted to dethrone George II and restore a Stuart monarch. Landing in Scotland, he garnered support from Highland clans who formed an army. Despite early victories, he was ultimately defeated by George II's forces at the Battle of Culloden in 1746. Charles fled back to Europe, and the clans lost much of their power. Clan chieftains who gained favor with the English king became landlords, while clansmen became tenants paying for the land they used.

This defeat led to the "Highland Clearances," a period when Scottish landlords cleared small farms, or "crofts," to make way for large flocks of sheep and cattle. Evictions became widespread in the early 19th century, prompting many Scots to emigrate to North America.

Robert Burns (1759–96)

Robert Burns, often referred to as "The Bard," was a renowned Scottish poet who wrote in Scots (English with Scottish influences) and standard English. He is celebrated for his revisions of traditional folk songs, where he frequently altered or added lyrics. Burns is especially famous for his song "Auld Lang Syne," which is widely sung during New Year's celebrations, known as "Hogmanay" in Scotland.

The Enlightenment

During the 18th century, known as the Enlightenment, groundbreaking ideas in politics, philosophy, and science emerged. Scotland was a hub for many influential thinkers of this era. Adam Smith developed economic theories that remain relevant, and David Hume's insights into human nature continue to shape philosophical discussions. James Watt's innovations in steam power were pivotal in advancing the Industrial Revolution. A fundamental Enlightenment principle was that individuals should be free to hold their own political and religious beliefs without government interference, a principle that remains vital in the UK today.

The Industrial Revolution

Before the 18th century, agriculture was the main source of employment in Britain, complemented by cottage industries where people produced goods like cloth and lace from their homes. The Industrial Revolution, spanning the 18th and 19th centuries, marked a period of rapid industrialisation, with Britain leading the way in large-scale industrial development. Advances in machinery and steam power were key to this transformation, mechanizing agriculture and manufacturing and boosting efficiency and output.

The rise of factories, which needed coal and other raw materials, prompted a migration from rural areas to urban centers for work in mining and manufacturing. A major breakthrough during this time was the Bessemer process, which enabled the mass production of steel, fueling growth in shipbuilding and railways. As manufacturing became the dominant employment sector, working conditions were harsh, with long hours, unsafe environments, and child labor prevalent due to the lack of protective laws.

To support the burgeoning industries, Britain constructed canals to transport raw materials and goods between factories, towns, and ports. Concurrently, Britain expanded its global influence, with Captain James Cook mapping Australia, Canada coming under British control, and the East India Company establishing dominance in India. This expansion facilitated the import of goods such as sugar, tobacco, textiles, tea, and spices from North America, the West Indies, India, and Indonesia, though it also led to conflicts with other expanding nations like France.

Richard Arkwright (1732–1792)

Born in 1732, Richard Arkwright started his career as a barber but transitioned to the textile industry, where he made significant innovations. He enhanced the carding machine and pioneered horse-driven spinning mills, boosting production efficiency. Later, he utilised the steam engine to power his machinery, and he is well-remembered for his effective factory management.

Sake Dean Mahomet (1759–1851)

Mahomet, born in 1759 in Bengal, India, grew up in the region before serving in the Bengal army. He arrived in Britain in 1782 and later moved to Ireland, where he married an Irish woman named Jane Daly in 1786. Returning to England at the turn of the century, he opened the Hindoostane Coffee House in George Street, London, in 1810, marking the first Indian restaurant in Britain. Mahomet and his wife also introduced the practice of "shampooing," an Indian head massage technique, to the British public.

The Slave Trade

The expansion of British commerce and wealth during this period was partly fueled by the growing slave trade. Although slavery was illegal in Britain itself, by the 18th century, it had become a prominent industry overseas, predominantly controlled by

Britain and its American colonies. Slaves, mostly from West Africa, were transported under horrific conditions on British ships to America and the Caribbean, where they were forced to work on tobacco and sugar plantations. The living and working conditions were inhumane, leading many slaves to attempt escape or rebellion.

Despite this, significant opposition to the slave trade existed in Britain. The Quakers were among the first to form anti-slavery groups in the late 1700s, actively petitioning Parliament for abolition. William Wilberforce, an evangelical Christian and MP, was pivotal in shifting public opinion and advocating for legislative change. His efforts, alongside other abolitionists, led to the abolition of the slave trade in British ships and ports in 1807 and the eventual end of slavery throughout the British Empire with the Emancipation Act of 1833. The Royal Navy also played a crucial role in intercepting slave ships, freeing enslaved people, and prosecuting slave traders.

Following the abolition of slavery, Britain brought in two million Indian and Chinese workers to fill the labor gap. These workers were employed on sugar plantations in the Caribbean, in South African mines, on railways in East Africa, and in the army in Kenya.

The American War of Independence

In the 1760s, the British colonies in North America were well-established, prosperous, and enjoyed significant autonomy. Many of the colonists had settled there seeking religious freedom and were well-educated, embracing ideas of liberty.

However, the British government's attempts to impose taxes on the colonies were perceived as an infringement on their freedoms, leading to widespread protests under the banner "no taxation without representation" in the British Parliament. Despite some attempts at compromise, such as repealing certain taxes, tensions between the British government and the colonies escalated. This friction eventually resulted in armed conflict, and in 1776, the 13 American colonies declared their independence, asserting their right to self-governance. After a prolonged struggle, the colonies defeated the British forces, and Britain officially recognised their independence in 1783.

War with France

In the 18th century, Britain was involved in several conflicts with France. In 1789, France experienced a revolution and subsequently declared war on Britain, a conflict that persisted under Napoleon Bonaparte's leadership. The British navy faced off against combined French and Spanish fleets, achieving a decisive victory at the Battle of Trafalgar in 1805.

Admiral Horatio Nelson, who commanded the British fleet, died in the battle. A monument in his honour, Nelson's Column, stands in Trafalgar Square in London, and his flagship, HMS Victory, is a renowned attraction in Portsmouth. Additionally, the British army fought against the French, and the French Wars concluded in 1815 when the Duke of Wellington defeated Napoleon at the Battle of Waterloo. Wellington, known as the Iron Duke, later served as Prime Minister.

The Union Flag

In 1801, the Act of Union united Ireland with England, Scotland, and Wales to form the United Kingdom of Great Britain and Ireland. To represent this union, a new version of the national flag, known as the Union Flag or Union Jack, was introduced. This flag combines the crosses of England, Scotland, and Ireland: the red cross of St. George (patron saint of England) on a white background; the white saltire of St. Andrew (patron saint of Scotland) on a blue background; and the red saltire of St. Patrick (patron saint of Ireland) on a white background. The Welsh dragon, featured on the Welsh flag, is not included in the Union Flag because Wales was already part of England when the original Union Flag was designed in 1606. Today, the Union Flag remains the official flag of the UK.

The Victorian Age

Queen Victoria began her reign in 1837 at the age of 18 and remained on the throne until 1901, ruling for nearly 64 years. This period is known as the Victorian Era, during which Britain significantly expanded its global influence and power. Domestically, the rise of the middle class became notable, and various reformers worked to improve the living conditions of the poor.

The British Empire

During the Victorian era, the British Empire expanded significantly to include territories such as India, Australia, and large portions of Africa, becoming the largest empire in the world with a population estimated at over 400 million. The British government actively encouraged emigration, leading around 13 million Britons to move overseas between 1853 and 1913. Simultaneously, Britain saw an influx of immigrants from various regions, including Russian and Polish Jews fleeing persecution, as well as individuals from other parts of the British Empire. Many Jewish immigrants settled in London's East End, as well as in Manchester and Leeds.

Trade and Industry

During the Victorian era, Britain thrived as a leading trading nation, driven by policies that promoted free trade and eliminated import taxes. The 1846 repeal of the Corn Laws, for example, lowered grain prices and stimulated British industry.

Factory working conditions improved gradually, thanks to laws limiting women and children to a maximum of 10 working hours per day and initiatives to build better housing for workers.

In the 19th century, British industry led the world, producing over half of the globe's iron, coal, and cotton cloth. The UK also emerged as a hub for financial services, including insurance and banking. The Great Exhibition of 1851, held in the Crystal Palace in Hyde Park, featured a wide array of exhibits, from large machinery to handmade goods, with a strong emphasis on British-made items.

Transportation saw major advancements, notably with the expansion of railways driven by the innovations of George and Robert Stephenson. This period also witnessed significant engineering feats, including the construction of iconic bridges by Isambard Kingdom Brunel, enhancing the movement of goods and people across the country and the British Empire.

Isambard Kingdom Brunel (1806–59)

Isambard Kingdom Brunel, born in Portsmouth, was a celebrated engineer recognised for his work on tunnels, bridges, railway lines, and ships. Among his most significant accomplishments was the construction of the Great Western Railway, the first major railway in Britain, extending from Paddington Station in London to the South West of England, the West Midlands, and Wales. Many of Brunel's bridges remain in use today and are regarded as iconic landmarks.

The Crimean War

From 1853 to 1856, the Crimean War took place, with Britain aligning with Turkey and France against Russia. This conflict was the first to receive extensive media coverage, including news reports and photographs. Unfortunately, soldiers endured harsh conditions, and many perished from illnesses acquired in hospitals rather than from battlefield injuries. To recognise acts of bravery during the war, Queen Victoria established the Victoria Cross medal.

Florence Nightingale (1820–1910)

Florence Nightingale, born to English parents in Italy, trained as a nurse in Germany at the age of 31. In 1854, she travelled to Turkey to work in military hospitals, caring for soldiers during the Crimean War. Along with her team of nurses, she improved hospital conditions and significantly reduced the mortality rate.

In 1860, Nightingale established the Nightingale Training School for Nurses at St Thomas' Hospital in London, the first of its kind and still operational today. Many of the nursing practices she developed continue to be used, and she is widely regarded as the founder of modern nursing.

Ireland in the 19th Century

Conditions in Ireland during the 19th century were notably harsher than in the rest of the UK. Around two-thirds of the population depended on farming, often on small plots of land, and many relied heavily on potatoes as a staple food. However, a catastrophic potato crop failure in the mid-century led to a devastating famine, which caused the deaths of around a million people from disease and starvation and prompted an additional one-and-a-half million to emigrate, with many heading to the United States or England.

By 1861, large Irish communities had established themselves in cities such as Liverpool, London, Manchester, and Glasgow. Throughout the century, the Irish Nationalist movement gained momentum. Some groups, like the Fenians, pursued complete independence for Ireland, while others, including Charles Stuart Parnell, championed "Home Rule", which aimed for Ireland to have its own parliament while remaining part of the United Kingdom.

The Right to Vote

During the 19th century, the growing influence of the middle class in prosperous industrial towns and cities led to demands for greater political power. The Reform Act of 1832 expanded the electorate and eliminated pocket and rotten boroughs. A "pocket" borough referred to one where the landowner had complete control over its parliamentary representation, while "rotten" boroughs were constituencies with very few inhabitants that still maintained parliamentary representation.

The Act increased parliamentary seats for towns and cities, shifting political power away from rural areas. However, voting remained limited to property owners, excluding working-class citizens from the electorate.

The Chartist movement emerged, advocating for voting rights for the working class and those without property, presenting petitions to Parliament. While initially unsuccessful, the Reform Act of 1867 created additional urban parliamentary seats and reduced property ownership requirements for voting. Despite these changes, most men and all women still lacked voting rights.

As the number of voters increased, politicians recognised the need to appeal to a broader electorate. Political parties began forming organisations to connect with ordinary voters. Universal suffrage, granting voting rights to all adults regardless of gender, was achieved in the following century.

In the 19th century, women in Britain had fewer rights than men. Upon marriage, a woman's earnings, property, and money automatically belonged to her husband until 1870. Legislation in 1870 and 1882 allowed married women to retain their earnings and property. The late 19th and early 20th centuries saw growing numbers of women campaigning for expanded rights, notably through the women's suffrage movement, with activists known as "suffragettes" advocating for the right to vote.

Emmeline Pankhurst (1858–1928)

Emmeline Pankhurst, born in Manchester in 1858, founded the Women's Franchise League in 1889, which sought to secure the vote for married women in local elections. In 1903, she co-founded the Women's Social and Political Union (WSPU), a group of suffragettes known for their militant tactics. The WSPU employed civil disobedience, including chaining themselves to railings, smashing windows, and committing arson.

Many suffragettes, including Pankhurst, engaged in hunger strikes to protest for their cause. The Representation of the People Act, passed in 1918, granted women over 30 the right to vote and stand for Parliament, recognising their contributions during the First World War. Just before Pankhurst's death in 1928, the voting age for women was equalised with men at 21.

The Future of the Empire

In the late 19th century, despite its continued expansion until the 1920s, debates about the future of the British Empire began to emerge. While some viewed expansion as beneficial for Britain, enhancing trade and commerce, others argued that the Empire had overextended itself and that conflicts across its vast territories were straining resources. Nonetheless, many Britons continued to see the Empire as a positive force in the world.

The Boer War, fought between 1899 and 1902 in South Africa between the British and the Dutch settlers known as the Boers, intensified these debates. The Boers' fierce resistance led to a protracted conflict, resulting in significant casualties from both fighting and disease. As public sympathy for the Boers grew, questions about the Empire's sustainability became more prominent. Over time, as various parts of the Empire gained increasing autonomy, the transition to a Commonwealth of Nations unfolded, culminating in the granting of independence to many countries by the latter half of the 20th century.

Rudyard Kipling (1865–1936)

Born in India in 1865, Rudyard Kipling lived in India, the UK, and the USA throughout his life. He authored books and poems set in both India and the UK, often depicting the British Empire in a positive light. Kipling received the Nobel Prize in Literature in 1907 and is renowned for his works such as *Just So Stories* and *The Jungle Book*, which continue to be widely read.

Revision Questions

Q1. Where was Rudyard Kipling born?
A) China
B) India
C) Ireland
D) USA

Q2. Who founded the Women's Franchise League in 1889?
A) Emmeline Pankhurst
B) J.K. Rowling
C) Margaret Thatcher
D) Queen Victoria

Q3. In which overseas war was Florence Nightingale integral to reducing the mortality rate?
A) World War I
B) World War II
C) The Boer War
D) The Crimean War

Q4. Isambard Kingdom Brunel was a prominent:
A) Poet
B) Musician
C) Engineer
D) Cricket player

Q5. Which decisive victory did the British navy achieve against a combined fleet of French and Spanish ships in the year 1805?
A) The Battle of Trafalgar
B) The Battle of the Bulge
C) The Battle of Mayfair
D) Pearl Harbor

Q6. True or false? A "rotten" borough is a constituency with parliamentary representation but very few inhabitants.

Q7. What was the impact of the Boer War on public opinion about the British Empire?
A) It strengthened support for the Empire.
B) It had no effect on public opinion.
C) It led to increased public sympathy for the Boers and doubts about the Empire.

D) It encouraged expansion of the Empire.

Q8. Which two major political factions emerged in Parliament, signifying the beginning of party politics?
A) Whigs and Hats
B) Whigs and Tories
C) Democrats and Liberals
D) Republicans and Democrats

Q9. Which famous building housed the Great Exhibition of 1851?
A) Buckingham Palace
B) The Crystal Palace
C) The British Museum
D) The Tower of London

Q10. Sake Dean Mohomet opened which of the following after arriving in Britain from India?
A) A shampoo clinic
B) An Indian restaurant
C) A fish n' chip shop
D) A takeaway restaurant

Answers

Q1. Where was Rudyard Kipling born?
Answer: B – India

Q2. Who founded the Women's Franchise League in 1889?
Answer: A – Emmeline Pankhurst

Q3. In which overseas war was Florence Nightingale integral to reducing the mortality rate?
Answer: D – The Crimean War

Q4. Isambard Kingdom Brunel was a prominent:
Answer: C – Engineer

Q5. Which decisive victory did the British navy achieve against a combined fleet of French and Spanish ships in the year 1805?
Answer: A – The Battle of Trafalgar

Q6. True or false? A "rotten" borough is a constituency with parliamentary representation but very few inhabitants.
Answer: True

Q7. What was the impact of the Boer War on public opinion about the British Empire?
Answer: C – It led to increased public sympathy for the Boers and doubts about the Empire.

Q8. Which two major political factions emerged in Parliament, signifying the beginning of party politics?
Answer: B – Whigs and Tories

Q9. Which famous building housed the Great Exhibition of 1851?
Answer: B – The Crystal Palace

Q10. Sake Dean Mohomet opened which of the following after arriving in Britain from India?
Answer: B – An Indian restaurant

The 20th Century

The First World War

The early 20th century was marked by optimism and progress in Britain. With its vast empire, powerful navy, thriving industry, and robust political institutions, Britain was seen as a global superpower. During this period, significant social advancements were made, including financial support for the unemployed, old-age pensions, and free school meals. Workplace safety was improved, town planning regulations were enforced to curb slum development, and enhanced support was provided to mothers and children following divorce or separation. Local government became more democratic, and for the first time, Members of Parliament were paid, making public service more accessible.

However, this era of progress was disrupted by the outbreak of the First World War in 1914. The assassination of Archduke Franz Ferdinand of Austria triggered the war, but underlying factors such as nationalism, militarism, imperialism, and the alignment of major European powers into opposing alliances created the conditions for conflict.

Though the war was primarily centred in Europe, it was a global conflict involving nations worldwide. The British Empire, including over a million Indian soldiers, fought alongside the Allied Powers, which included France, Russia, Japan, and Serbia, against the Central Powers—Germany, the Austro-Hungarian Empire, the Ottoman Empire, and Bulgaria. The war caused immense casualties, with over two million British soldiers affected. Notably, the British attack on the Somme in July 1916 resulted in approximately 60,000 British casualties on the first day alone.

The war concluded on 11 November 1918, at 11.00 am, with victory for Britain and its allies.

The Partition of Ireland

In 1913, the British government promised to grant Home Rule to Ireland, allowing it to have its own parliament and self-govern while remaining part of the UK. However, this proposal was met with strong opposition from Protestants in Northern Ireland, who threatened armed resistance.

The onset of World War I led the British government to delay implementing these changes in Ireland, but Irish Nationalists were unwilling to wait. In 1916, the Easter Rising erupted in Dublin as a rebellion against British rule. The leaders of the uprising were executed under military law, sparking a guerrilla war against British forces in Ireland. By 1921, a peace treaty was signed, leading to the division of Ireland into two separate entities. The six predominantly Protestant counties in the north became Northern Ireland, remaining part of the UK, while the rest of Ireland formed the Irish Free State. The Irish Free State established its own government and became a republic in 1949.

Despite this resolution, many people in both parts of Ireland opposed the division and sought a unified, independent nation. This disagreement resulted in years of conflict and a violent campaign in Northern Ireland, known as "the Troubles."

The Inter-War Period

In the 1920s, living conditions in the UK saw significant improvements. Public housing upgrades and the construction of new homes enriched various towns and cities. However, the onset of the Great Depression in 1929 brought widespread unemployment to parts of the country. The impact of the Depression in the 1930s was uneven: while traditional heavy industries like shipbuilding struggled, emerging sectors such as the automobile and aviation industries thrived. As prices fell, those with jobs had more disposable income. Car ownership surged from 1 million to 2 million between 1930 and 1939, and many new houses were built.

The 1930s also marked a period of cultural advancement, with influential writers like Graham Greene and Evelyn Waugh rising to prominence and economist John Maynard Keynes publishing groundbreaking economic theories. The BBC made strides in media, starting radio broadcasts in 1922 and launching the world's first regular television service in 1936.

The Second World War

Adolf Hitler rose to power in Germany in 1933 with the goal of reversing the perceived injustices imposed on Germany by the Allies after World War I and expanding German territory. He began renegotiating treaties, ramping up military production, and testing Germany's military strength in neighbouring countries. Initially, the British government sought to avoid conflict, but when Hitler invaded Poland in 1939, Britain and France declared war to halt his aggression.

The ensuing conflict, known as World War II, pitted the Allies against the Axis powers, which included fascist Germany, Italy, and the Empire of Japan. Key Allied nations included the UK, France, Poland, Australia, New Zealand, Canada, and the Union of South Africa.

Hitler swiftly occupied Austria, invaded Czechoslovakia, and then took control of Belgium and the Netherlands before defeating Allied forces and advancing through France in 1940. During this critical period, Winston Churchill became Prime Minister and assumed leadership of Britain's war efforts.

As France fell, Britain executed a massive naval operation to evacuate over 300,000 soldiers from the beaches around Dunkirk. Many civilian volunteers in small boats joined the effort, assisting the Navy in rescuing troops. Although the evacuation involved significant losses, it was deemed a success and allowed Britain to continue resisting the Germans, inspiring the term "the Dunkirk spirit."

From late June 1940 until the German invasion of the Soviet Union in June 1941, Britain and its Empire stood nearly alone against Nazi Germany. Hitler aimed to invade Britain but first needed to gain control of the air. The Germans launched an extensive air campaign, but the British, with their fighter planes, notably the Spitfire and Hurricane, managed to win the pivotal Battle of Britain during the summer of 1940.

Despite this crucial victory, the German air force continued nighttime bombings of London and other British cities, known as "the Blitz," causing extensive damage in places like Coventry. Nonetheless, the UK demonstrated remarkable resilience during this period, and the term "the Blitz spirit" continues to symbolise the nation's unity and determination in the face of adversity.

Winston Churchill (1874–1965)

Winston Churchill was a Conservative MP, soldier, and journalist who became Prime Minister in May 1940. During a period of severe hardship, he refused to surrender to the Nazis, offering inspiration to the British people. Although he lost the General Election in 1945, he returned to the role of Prime Minister in 1951. Churchill served as a Member of Parliament until he retired after the 1964 General Election and was given a state funeral upon his death in 1965. Widely admired, he was voted the greatest Briton of all time by the public in 2002.

Churchill's wartime speeches became legendary, with memorable lines such as "I have nothing to offer but blood, toil, tears and sweat," "We shall fight on the beaches…," and "Never in the field of human conflict was so much owed by so many to so few."

While Britain defended itself against the Nazis, the British military was also engaged on multiple other fronts. The Japanese defeated British forces in Singapore and subsequently occupied Burma, threatening India. The United States entered the war following the Japanese attack on Pearl Harbor in December 1941. In the same year, Hitler launched a massive invasion of the Soviet Union, leading to significant casualties on both sides. Despite initial setbacks, German forces were eventually pushed back by the Soviets, marking a crucial turning point in the conflict.

The Allies gradually gained the upper hand, securing important victories in North Africa and Italy. With German losses in the Soviet Union and increasing American support, the Allies were able to launch attacks against Hitler's forces in Western Europe. On June 6, 1944, Allied troops landed in Normandy in what is commonly known as "D-Day." Following their success on the Normandy beaches, the Allies advanced through France and into Germany, culminating in the defeat of the Germans in May 1945.

The war in the Pacific ended in August 1945 when the United States dropped atomic bombs on Hiroshima and Nagasaki. The scientists who first split the atom, including Ernest Rutherford, worked at Manchester and Cambridge Universities and later contributed to the Manhattan Project, where the atomic bomb was ultimately developed.

Alexander Fleming (1881–1955)

After relocating to London as a teenager, Alexander Fleming became a qualified doctor and started researching influenza in 1928. During his studies, he discovered penicillin, which was later developed into a practical drug by scientists Howard Florey and Ernst Chain.

By the 1940s, penicillin was being mass-produced and widely used to treat bacterial infections. Fleming was honored with the Nobel Prize in Medicine in 1945 for his groundbreaking discovery. Today, penicillin continues to be a crucial antibiotic in the treatment of bacterial infections.

Revision Questions

Q1. What event triggered the outbreak of the First World War in 1914?

A) The sinking of the Lusitania
B) The assassination of Archduke Franz Ferdinand
C) The signing of the Treaty of Versailles
D) The invasion of Poland

Q2. What significant political change did the British government promise Ireland in 1913?

A) A separate parliament and self-governance
B) Full independence
C) Equal rights for all citizens
D) Union with Scotland

Q3. Which Irish uprising occurred in 1916 against British rule?

A) The Great Rebellion
B) The Easter Rising
C) The Dublin Revolt
D) The Ulster Uprising

Q4. Which British Prime Minister became famous for his speeches during the Second World War?

A) Neville Chamberlain
B) Clement Attlee
C) Winston Churchill
D) Stanley Baldwin

Q5. What was the significance of the Battle of Britain in 1940?

A) It marked the end of the war
B) It was a crucial aerial battle won by the British
C) It resulted in the German invasion of France
D) It was a naval battle in the Atlantic

Q6. What was the name given to the extensive German bombing campaign of British cities during World War II?

A) The Blitz
B) Operation Sea Lion
C) The Luftwaffe Offensive
D) The Blitzkrieg

Q7. Who discovered penicillin and won the Nobel Prize in Medicine in 1945?

A) Howard Florey
B) Ernst Chain

C) Alexander Fleming
D) John Maynard Keynes

Answers

Q1. What event triggered the outbreak of the First World War in 1914?

Answer: B – The assassination of Archduke Franz Ferdinand

Q2. What significant political change did the British government promise Ireland in 1913?

Answer: A – A separate parliament and self-governance

Note: The British government promised Ireland Home Rule, which included a separate parliament and self-governance.

Q3. Which Irish uprising occurred in 1916 against British rule?

Answer: B – The Easter Rising

Q4. Which British Prime Minister became famous for his speeches during the Second World War?

Answer: C – Winston Churchill

Q5. What was the significance of the Battle of Britain in 1940?

Answer: B – It was a crucial aerial battle won by the British

Q6. What was the name given to the extensive German bombing campaign of British cities during World War II?

Answer: A – The Blitz

Q7. Who discovered penicillin and won the Nobel Prize in Medicine in 1945?

Answer: C – Alexander Fleming

Britain Since 1945

The Welfare State

After the Second World War, the UK faced economic exhaustion and a strong desire for change. In 1945, the Labour Party, led by Clement Attlee, won the election. Attlee promised to implement the welfare state outlined in the Beveridge Report. By 1948, Aneurin (Nye) Bevan had established the National Health Service (NHS), which provided free healthcare for all. Additionally, a system of benefits was introduced to ensure social security, and the government nationalised key industries, including railways, coal mines, gas, water, and electricity supplies.

During this era, the UK granted self-government to former colonies, developed its own atomic bomb, and joined the North Atlantic Treaty Organisation (NATO). The 1950s saw economic recovery and rising prosperity, with Harold Macmillan leading the Conservative government from 1951 to 1964. Macmillan supported decolonisation and the independence of former Empire nations.

Clement Attlee, born in London in 1883, served as Deputy Prime Minister in Winston Churchill's wartime coalition before becoming Prime Minister in 1945. He led the Labour Party for two decades and was instrumental in implementing Beveridge's plans for an enhanced welfare state, including nationalizing major industries, establishing the NHS, and improving workers' conditions.

William Beveridge (1879–1963)

Lord William Beveridge, a British economist and social reformer, is renowned for his groundbreaking 1942 report, "Social Insurance and Allied Services," commonly known as the Beveridge Report. Before this, Beveridge had a brief tenure as a Liberal MP and later led the Liberals in the House of Lords. Commissioned by the government in 1941 during World War II, the report proposed solutions to address the five "Giant Evils" of Want, Disease, Ignorance, Squalor, and Idleness. His recommendations played a crucial role in shaping the modern welfare state.

R A Butler (1902–1982)

Richard Austen Butler, who later became known as Lord Butler, was born in 1902 and began his parliamentary career with the Conservative Party in 1923. He held several key positions before being appointed Minister of Education in 1941. During his time in office, he was responsible for introducing the Education Act of 1944, commonly referred to as "The Butler Act." This legislation made secondary education free for all children in England and Wales and has been a cornerstone of the British education system ever since.

Dylan Thomas (1914–1953)

Dylan Thomas was a Welsh writer and poet renowned for his captivating public readings and performances, including those for the BBC. His most celebrated works include the radio play *Under Milk Wood*, which premiered posthumously in 1954, and the poem "Do Not Go Gentle into That Good Night," penned for his father in 1952 as he was dying. Thomas passed away at the age of 39 in New York, and his birthplace, Swansea, honours his legacy with several memorials, including a statue and the Dylan Thomas Centre.

Migration in Post-War Britain

After World War II, Britain faced a massive task of reconstruction amid severe labor shortages. To address this, the British government actively encouraged workers from Ireland and other European countries to come to the UK. In 1948, invitations were also extended to people from the West Indies to assist with rebuilding efforts.

Throughout the 1950s, the UK continued to experience labor shortages and further immigration was promoted for economic reasons. Many industries began recruiting workers from abroad, with advertisements and recruitment centers established in the West Indies to find bus drivers. Additionally, textile and engineering firms from northern England and the Midlands sent agents to India and Pakistan to recruit workers. Over the next 25 years, individuals from the West Indies, India, Pakistan, and later Bangladesh, moved to the UK to work and settle.

Social Change in the 1960s

The 1960s, often called "the Swinging Sixties," was a decade of profound social transformation in Britain. It saw the rise of influential British fashion, cinema, and music, with iconic bands like The Beatles and The Rolling Stones leading the cultural charge. Economic prosperity grew, boosting car ownership and consumer goods purchases.

The era was also marked by significant social reforms, including the liberalisation of divorce and abortion laws in England, Wales, and Scotland. Women's roles in the workplace improved with new legislation ensuring equal pay and combatting gender discrimination.

Technological advancements were notable, highlighted by the development of Concorde, the world's only supersonic commercial airliner. In architecture, the use of high-rise buildings, concrete, and steel became more common.

Towards the end of the decade, the UK government introduced new immigration restrictions, requiring immigrants to have a strong connection to Britain through birth or ancestry. This led to a decline in migration from the West Indies, India, Pakistan, and Bangladesh. However, in the early 1970s, the UK accepted 28,000 people of Indian origin who had been expelled from Uganda.

Major British Inventions of the 20th Century

Britain has made many significant contributions to global innovation. Notable examples from the 20th century include:

Television: Developed by John Logie Baird, a Scottish inventor, who made the first television broadcast between London and Glasgow in 1932.

Radar: Invented by Sir Robert Watson-Watt, a Scottish scientist, who demonstrated the first successful radar test in 1935 by detecting enemy aircraft using radio waves.

Radio Telescope: Sir Bernard Lovell, a British astronomer, built the world's largest radio telescope at Jodrell Bank in Cheshire, which remains in use today and contributed significantly to astronomical research.

Turing Machine: Alan Turing, a British mathematician, created the theoretical Turing machine in the 1930s, which laid the groundwork for modern computer science.

Insulin: Co-discovered by John MacLeod, a Scottish physician, insulin revolutionised the treatment of diabetes.

DNA Structure: The double helix structure of DNA was uncovered in 1953 through research at British universities in London and Cambridge. Francis Crick, a British scientist, was awarded the Nobel Prize for this groundbreaking discovery.

Jet Engine: Developed by Sir Frank Whittle, a British Royal Air Force engineer officer, in the 1930s, the jet engine transformed aviation.

Hovercraft: Invented by Sir Christopher Cockerell in the 1950s, the hovercraft is a versatile vehicle capable of traveling over various surfaces.

Concorde: The supersonic passenger aircraft developed jointly by Britain and France, which first flew in 1969 and began commercial service in 1976 before being retired in 2003.

ATM: The cash-dispensing automatic teller machine (ATM), or "cashpoint," was invented by James Goodfellow, with the first machine installed by Barclays Bank in Enfield, London, in 1967.

IVF: Pioneered by Sir Robert Edwards and Patrick Steptoe, this in-vitro fertilisation technique led to the birth of the world's first "test-tube baby" in Oldham, Lancashire, in 1978.

Cloning: In 1996, Sir Ian Wilmut and Keith Campbell led the team that successfully cloned Dolly the sheep, advancing research in cloning and its potential applications.

MRI Scanner: Co-invented by Sir Peter Mansfield, this magnetic resonance imaging scanner has revolutionised medical diagnostics by providing detailed, non-invasive images of the body's internal structures.

World Wide Web: Invented by Sir Tim Berners-Lee, the web was first used to transfer information on December 25, 1990, fundamentally transforming how we access and share information.

Problems in the Economy in the 1970s

In the late 1970s, Britain experienced an economic downturn that marked the end of the post-war boom. Prices for goods and raw materials surged, and the pound's exchange rate became unstable, leading to a troubled balance of payments as imports exceeded exports in cost.

The period was also marked by widespread strikes across various industries and services, straining relations between trade unions and the government. There was a growing perception that the unions had become overly influential, negatively impacting the country.

Northern Ireland faced severe unrest and violence during the 1970s. In 1972, the UK government suspended the Northern Ireland Parliament and took over direct governance of the region. The conflict, known as "the Troubles," persisted for decades and resulted in approximately 3,000 deaths.

Mary Peters (born 1939)

Mary Peters, originally from Manchester, relocated to Northern Ireland as a child. Demonstrating exceptional talent in athletics, she won an Olympic gold medal in the pentathlon in 1972. Following her athletic success, Peters dedicated herself to raising funds for local sports and took on the role of team manager for the British women's Olympic team. She remains an advocate for sports and tourism in Northern Ireland and was appointed Dame of the British Empire in 2000 in recognition of her contributions.

Europe and the Common Market

The European Economic Community (EEC) was founded in 1957 by West Germany, France, Belgium, Italy, Luxembourg, and the Netherlands. Although initially hesitant, the UK joined the EEC in 1973. Despite being a full member of the European Union, the UK opted not to adopt the Euro currency.

Margaret Thatcher (1925–2013)

Margaret Thatcher, born in Grantham, Lincolnshire, was the daughter of a grocer. She trained as a chemist and lawyer before becoming a Conservative MP in 1959. In 1970, she was appointed Secretary of State for Education and Science. By 1975, she had been elected Leader of the Conservative Party and Leader of the Opposition.

Thatcher became the UK's first female Prime Minister after the Conservative Party's victory in the 1979 General Election, serving until 1990. Her tenure marked her as the longest-serving Prime Minister of the 20th century. She implemented major economic reforms, including the privatisation of state-owned industries and the introduction of legal restrictions on trade unions. Her policies fostered the growth of the City of London as a global financial hub, though traditional industries like coal mining and shipbuilding faced decline.

Thatcher collaborated closely with US President Ronald Reagan and played a key role in acknowledging the Soviet Union's changing leadership, contributing to the end of the Cold War. In 1982, during her premiership, Argentina's invasion of the Falkland Islands led to a successful British naval operation to reclaim the territory. Thatcher was succeeded by John Major, who significantly contributed to the Northern Ireland peace process.

Roald Dahl (1916–1990)

Roald Dahl, born in Wales to Norwegian parents, served in the Royal Air Force during World War II. He began publishing books and short stories in the 1940s, gaining fame for his engaging stories for both children and adults. Among his most celebrated works are *Charlie and the Chocolate Factory* and *George's Marvellous Medicine*, both of which have been adapted into successful films.

Labour Government From 1997-2010

Tony Blair's Labour Party secured victory in the 1997 general election. During their time in power, they established a Scottish Parliament with substantial legislative authority and a Welsh Assembly with more limited powers but significant control over public services.

The Blair government also advanced the peace process in Northern Ireland, leading to the signing of the Good Friday Agreement in 1998. The Northern Ireland Assembly was elected in 1999 but was suspended in 2002 and only reinstated in 2007. As of now, most paramilitary groups in Northern Ireland have decommissioned their weapons and remain inactive. Gordon Brown succeeded Tony Blair as Prime Minister in 2007.

Conflicts in Afghanistan & Iraq

In the 1990s, the UK was a key member of the coalition forces that liberated Kuwait after Iraq's invasion in 1990 and participated in the conflict in the Former Republic of Yugoslavia. Since the year 2000, British armed forces have been deeply involved in combating international terrorism and addressing the proliferation of weapons of mass destruction, with significant operations in Afghanistan and Iraq. British combat troops withdrew from Iraq in 2009 and from Afghanistan in 2014.

Government From 2010 Onwards

In the General Election of May 2010, no party in the UK secured an outright majority for the first time since February 1974. Consequently, the Conservative (Tory) Party and the Liberal Democrats formed a coalition government, with David Cameron, the leader of the Conservative Party, becoming Prime Minister.

In July 2016, Theresa May, also from the Conservative Party, succeeded David Cameron as Prime Minister after he resigned following the UK's vote to leave the European Union (Brexit). May triggered Article 50 to formally start the withdrawal process but faced challenges in securing parliamentary support for her Brexit deal, leading to delays and political impasse. She resigned as Conservative leader in July 2019 and was succeeded by Boris Johnson.

Boris Johnson, a prominent Brexit advocate and member of the Conservative Party, became Prime Minister in July 2019. He fulfilled his pledge to "get Brexit done" by negotiating a revised withdrawal agreement with the EU, which Parliament approved. The UK officially left the EU on January 31, 2020, entering a transition period that lasted until December 31, 2020, during which further discussions on future relations were held.

Liz Truss, another Conservative, took over as Prime Minister after Boris Johnson's resignation due to internal party issues. Her tenure was brief, lasting less than two months, as she resigned following internal party dissent over budgetary issues and a proposed ban on fracking, making her the shortest-serving Prime Minister in UK history.

On October 25, 2022, Rishi Sunak of the Conservative Party became Prime Minister, making him the first British Asian and the first Hindu to hold the office.

In the 2024 UK election, Keir Starmer was elected as the next Prime Minister in what was a landslide victory for the Labour Party.

Revision Questions

Q1. In which election did no party win an absolute majority for the first time since February 1974?

A) 2005 General Election
B) 2010 General Election
C) 2015 General Election
D) 2019 General Election

Q2. Who became Prime Minister after David Cameron resigned following the EU Referendum in 2016?

A) Boris Johnson
B) Liz Truss
C) Theresa May
D) Rishi Sunak

Q3. What significant event led to Theresa May triggering Article 50?

A) The UK General Election
B) The result of the EU Referendum
C) The Conservative Party conference
D) The London Olympics

Q4. Who succeeded Theresa May as Prime Minister in July 2019?

A) David Cameron
B) Liz Truss
C) Boris Johnson
D) Rishi Sunak

Q5. What was Boris Johnson's key promise during his campaign for Prime Minister?

A) "Get Brexit done"
B) "Build back better"
C) "A fairer society for all"
D) "Increase public spending"

Q6. When did the UK officially leave the European Union?

A) January 1, 2010
B) January 31, 2020
C) December 31, 2024
D) January 31, 2001

Q7. Who was Roald Dahl?

A) A famous author
B) A prominent general
C) A former Prime Minister
D) A royal family member

Q8. True or false? Margaret Thatcher became the UK's second female Prime Minister after the Conservative Party's victory.

Answer: False

Q9. Which of the following is not a 20th Century British innovation?

A) The Turing machine
B) Insulin
C) Radio telescope
D) Wi-Fi technology

Q10. The 1960s was a decade of profound social transformation in Britain, known today as:

A) The Super Sixties
B) The Sweet Sixties
C) The Swinging Sixties
D) The Swooping Sixties

Answers

Q1. In which election did no party win an absolute majority for the first time since February 1974?

Answer: B – 2010 General Election

Note: In 2010, the UK saw a coalition government due to no party securing an outright majority.

Q2. Who became Prime Minister after David Cameron resigned following the EU Referendum in 2016?

Answer: C – Theresa May

Q3. What significant event led to Theresa May triggering Article 50?

Answer: B – The result of the EU Referendum

Note: Article 50 was triggered to start the formal process of the UK's withdrawal from the EU

Q4. Who succeeded Theresa May as Prime Minister in July 2019?

Answer: C – Boris Johnson

Q5. What was Boris Johnson's key promise during his campaign for Prime Minister?

Answer: A – "Get Brexit done"

Note: Johnson's campaign focused on completing the Brexit process.

Q6. When did the UK officially leave the European Union?

Answer: B – January 31, 2020

Q7. Who was Roald Dahl?

Answer: A – A famous author

Q8. True or false? Margaret Thatcher became the UK's second female Prime Minister after the Conservative Party's victory.

Answer: False

Thatcher was the UK's first female Prime Minister.

Q9. Which of the following is not a 20th Century British innovation?

Answer: D – Wi-Fi technology

Q10. The 1960s was a decade of profound social transformation in Britain, known today as:

Answer: C – The Swinging Sixties

Chapter 4: A Thriving Society & The UK Today

The UK Today

The ethnic and religious diversity of the UK has grown significantly over the past century due to post-war immigration. Today, nearly 10% of the population has a parent or grandparent born outside the UK. This has transformed the UK into a vibrant, multiethnic society with a rich cultural tapestry. This section offers insights into the various regions of the UK, important landmarks, notable traditions and customs, and popular events and activities.

The Nations of the UK

The United Kingdom is located in northwest Europe. The longest distance on the mainland, from John O'Groats on Scotland's northern coast to Land's End in the southwest of England, spans approximately 870 miles (about 1,400 kilometers). Although the majority of the population resides in urban areas, a considerable part of the country is rural. The countryside is a favored spot for vacations and recreational activities such as walking, camping, and fishing.

Capital Cities

London is the capital city of the UK

Edinburgh is the capital city of Scotland

Cardiff is the capital city of Wales

Belfast is the capital city of Northern Ireland

UK Currency

The official currency of the UK is the pound sterling, represented by the symbol £, and is divided into 100 pence. The currency includes coins in denominations of 1p, 2p, 5p, 10p, 20p, 50p, £1, and £2, as well as notes in £5, £10, £20, and £50. Scotland and Northern Ireland issue their own distinctive banknotes, which are valid across the UK, though businesses are not required to accept them.

Languages & Dialects

The UK features a rich tapestry of languages and dialects across its regions. English is spoken throughout the country with a range of accents and dialects. Welsh is a distinct language from English, spoken in Wales and taught in schools and universities. In Scotland, Gaelic is used in parts of the Highlands and Islands, while in Northern Ireland, some people speak Irish Gaelic.

Population

The UK's population has been steadily increasing over recent decades and is expected to keep growing. This growth is primarily driven by net migration and natural increase, which is the difference between births and deaths. According to the Office for National Statistics (ONS), the UK's population reached 67.026 million in mid-2021, marking a 5.9% rise from 63.326 million in mid-2011. The population distribution is uneven: England comprises approximately 84% of the total population, Wales about 4.5%, Scotland just over 8%, and Northern Ireland less than 3%. Recent growth has accelerated due to higher migration rates and increased life expectancy.

An Ageing Population

The UK population is benefiting from increased life expectancy due to improvements in healthcare and living standards. Consequently, there is now a higher number of people aged 85 and older than ever before. This demographic shift, however, places additional pressure on the costs associated with pensions and healthcare.

An Equal Society

In the UK, discrimination based on gender or marital status is prohibited by law. Men and women have equal rights to work, own property, marry, and divorce, and both parents share equal responsibility for their children if they are married.

Currently, women make up about half of the workforce in the UK. Girls often leave school with better qualifications than boys and more women than men pursue higher education. Employment opportunities for women have significantly expanded, with many now holding high-level positions across various sectors, including those traditionally dominated by men. Similarly, men are now employed in a broader range of roles.

It is also no longer expected that women should stay at home after having children. Many women continue to work while raising their families, and it is common for both partners to balance work and share childcare and household responsibilities.

Revision Questions

Q1. What is legally prohibited in the UK concerning gender and marital status?

A) Voting rights

B) Employment opportunities

C) Equal pay

D) Discrimination

Q2. What percentage of the UK workforce is currently made up of women?

A) About 25%

B) About 50%

C) About 75%

D) About 10%

Q3. Who is responsible for their children if the parents are married?

A) Only the mother

B) Only the father

C) Both parents

D) The grandparents

Q4. What is the official currency of the UK?

A) The Euro

B) The British Dollar

C) The Pound Sterling

D) BritCoin

Q5. What has seen significant improvement for women in the UK over recent years?

A) Educational achievements

B) Employment opportunities

C) Marital status

D) Housing options

Q6. What is not a distinct language native to the United Kingdom?

A) Welsh

B) Gaelic

C) English

D) Danish

Q7. What is the capital city of Northern Ireland?

A) Swansea

B) Belfast

C) London

D) Cardiff

Q8. What is the capital city of the UK?

A) Swansea

B) Belfast

C) London

D) Cardiff

Q9. What is the typical arrangement for both partners in modern households regarding work and chores?

A) One partner works while the other stays home

B) Both partners share work and household duties

C) One partner handles all childcare

D) Household chores are not shared

Q10. What is the capital city of Wales?

A) Swansea

B) Belfast

C) London

D) Cardiff

Answers

Q1. What is legally prohibited in the UK concerning gender and marital status?
Answer: D – Discrimination

Q2. What percentage of the UK workforce is currently made up of women?
Answer: B – About 50%

Q3. Who is responsible for their children if the parents are married?
Answer: C – Both parents

Q4. What is the official currency of the UK?
Answer: C – The Pound Sterling

Q5. What has seen significant improvement for women in the UK over recent years?
Answer: B – Employment opportunities

Q6. What is not a distinct language native to the United Kingdom?
Answer: D – Danish

Q7. What is the capital city of Northern Ireland?
Answer: B – Belfast

Q8. What is the capital city of the UK?
Answer: C – London

Q9. What is the typical arrangement for both partners in modern households regarding work and chores?
Answer: B – Both partners share work and household duties

Q10. What is the capital city of Wales?
Answer: D – Cardiff

Religion

Christian Churches

The relationship between church and state in England is defined by its constitutional framework. The official church is the Church of England, which is known internationally as the Anglican Church and as the Episcopal Church in Scotland and the United States. Established during the Reformation in the 1530s, this Protestant church is headed by the monarch, who acts as its supreme governor. The spiritual leader is the Archbishop of Canterbury. While the monarch has the authority to appoint the Archbishop and other senior church officials, these appointments are typically made by the Prime Minister and a church committee. Some bishops of the Church of England also have seats in the House of Lords.

In Scotland, the Church of Scotland serves as the national church. It follows a Presbyterian structure, led by ministers and elders. The Moderator, who is elected annually, chairs the General Assembly and represents the church publicly.

Wales and Northern Ireland do not have an established church. The UK also has various Protestant denominations, such as Baptists, Methodists, Presbyterians, and Quakers, alongside other Christian groups, with the Roman Catholic Church being the largest Christian denomination.

Patron Saints' Days

In England, Scotland, Wales, and Northern Ireland, each country has its own patron saint and dedicated celebration day. St David's Day, celebrated on March 1, honors Wales. St Patrick's Day, observed on March 17, is dedicated to Northern Ireland. England marks St George's Day on April 23, and Scotland celebrates St Andrew's Day on November 30.

While only Scotland and Northern Ireland officially recognise their patron saints' days as public holidays (with some exceptions in Scotland), these days are celebrated across the UK, especially in areas with significant Scottish, Northern Irish, and Irish communities. Although patron saints' days are not public holidays in England and Wales, they are still marked by parades and local festivals throughout both countries.

Revision Questions

Q1. Which patron saint's day is celebrated in Wales?
A) St George's Day
B) St Andrew's Day
C) St David's Day
D) St Patrick's Day

Q2. On which date is St Patrick's Day celebrated in Northern Ireland?
A) March 1
B) April 23
C) November 30
D) March 17

Q3. Which patron saint's day is observed in Scotland?
A) St David's Day
B) St George's Day
C) St Patrick's Day
D) St Andrew's Day

Q4. Which patron saint's day is celebrated on April 23?
A) St David's Day
B) St George's Day
C) St Patrick's Day
D) St Andrew's Day

Q5. Who is the head of the Church of England?
A) The monarch
B) The Pope
C) The Prime Minister
D) The Supreme Leader

Q6. What types of events are commonly held across the UK on patron saints' days?
A) National holidays
B) Public demonstrations
C) Parades and local festivals
D) State funerals

Q7. Which of the following countries does NOT officially recognise a patron saint's day as a public holiday?
A) Scotland
B) Northern Ireland
C) England
D) Wales

Answers

Q1. Which patron saint's day is celebrated in Wales?
Answer: C – St David's Day

Q2. On which date is St Patrick's Day celebrated in Northern Ireland?
Answer: D – March 17

Q3. Which patron saint's day is observed in Scotland?
Answer: D – St Andrew's Day

Q4. Which patron saint's day is celebrated on April 23?
Answer: B – St George's Day

Q5. Who is the head of the Church of England?
Answer: A – The Monarch

Q6. What types of events are commonly held across the UK on patron saints' days?
Answer: C – Parades and local festivals

Q7. Which of the following countries does NOT officially recognise a patron saint's day as a public holiday?
Answer: C – England

Customs & Traditions

The Main Christian Festivals

Christmas Day, celebrated on December 25th, marks the birth of Jesus Christ and is a public holiday in the UK. Many Christians attend church services on either Christmas Eve or Christmas Day. The holiday is traditionally spent with family at home, enjoying a festive meal that often includes roast turkey, Christmas pudding, and mince pies. Families exchange gifts, send cards, and decorate their homes, including setting up a Christmas tree. Children await visits from Father Christmas, also known as Santa Claus, who is believed to bring presents on Christmas Eve.

Boxing Day, observed on December 26th, is also a public holiday.

Easter, occurring in March or April, celebrates the death of Jesus Christ on Good Friday and his resurrection on Easter Sunday. Both Good Friday and Easter Monday are public holidays. The period leading up to Easter, known as Lent, lasts for 40 days and is a time for Christians to reflect and prepare for the celebration. Traditionally, this involves fasting, and today many people choose to give up a favorite food or treat.

Shrove Tuesday, or Pancake Day, is the day before Lent begins, when people traditionally eat pancakes to use up ingredients like eggs, fat, and milk before the fasting period. Lent begins on Ash Wednesday, when Christians attend church services and receive an ash cross on their foreheads as a symbol of repentance.

Easter is also celebrated by non-religious people, who often exchange chocolate Easter eggs as a symbol of new life.

Other Religious Festivals

Diwali, often called the "Festival of Lights," is celebrated by Hindus and Sikhs over five days in October or November. It marks the triumph of good over evil and the pursuit of knowledge. The festival's stories vary, but it is widely celebrated, with one of the largest observances held in Leicester.

Hanukkah, an eight-day Jewish festival, occurs in November or December and commemorates the Jewish struggle for religious freedom. Each night, a candle is lit on a menorah with eight branches, symbolizing the miracle of the oil that lasted eight days.

Eid al-Fitr signifies the end of Ramadan, a month of fasting for Muslims. The date varies each year, and Muslims express gratitude to Allah for the strength to complete their fast, participating in special prayers and communal meals.

Eid ul-Adha honors the Prophet Ibrahim's readiness to sacrifice his son as an act of devotion to God. Many Muslims sacrifice an animal during this festival, which must be done at a licensed slaughterhouse in the UK.

Vaisakhi, also known as Baisakhi, is a Sikh festival held on April 14 each year. It celebrates the formation of the Khalsa, the Sikh community, and is marked by vibrant parades, dancing, and singing.

Other Festivals & Traditions

New Year's Day, observed on January 1st, is a public holiday marking the start of the new year. Celebrations typically begin on the evening of December 31st, known as New Year's Eve.

In **Scotland**, December 31st is celebrated as **Hogmanay**, with January 2nd also being a public holiday. For many Scots, Hogmanay is even more significant than Christmas.

Valentine's Day, on February 14th, is dedicated to expressing love and affection. People exchange cards and gifts, and some may send anonymous cards to those they secretly admire.

April Fool's Day, on April 1st, is known for playing pranks and practical jokes until midday. Media outlets often feature fake stories as part of the day's festivities.

Mothering Sunday, or **Mother's Day**, falls three weeks before Easter. Children celebrate by sending cards and buying gifts for their mothers.

Father's Day, observed on the third Sunday of June, is a day when children show appreciation for their fathers through cards and gifts.

Halloween, on October 31st, has its roots in ancient pagan celebrations marking the onset of winter. Children often dress in spooky costumes for "trick or treat," asking for sweets to avoid pranks, and many people carve pumpkins into lanterns.

Bonfire Night (also known as Guy Fawkes Night), celebrated on November 5th, involves fireworks and bonfires across Great Britain. This event commemorates the thwarted 1605 plot by Guy Fawkes and his co-conspirators to blow up the Houses of Parliament.

Remembrance Day, observed on November 11th, honors those who died serving the UK and its allies. Initially marking the end of World War I on November 11, 1918, people wear poppies and observe a two-minute silence at 11:00 am.

Bank Holidays

Alongside the previously mentioned holidays, there are annual **bank holidays** when banks and many businesses close for the day. These holidays, which are secular in nature, usually take place at the start of May, late May or early June, and in August. Additionally, in **Northern Ireland**, the anniversary of the **Battle of the Boyne** in July is also recognised as a public holiday.

Revision Questions

Q1. What type of holidays are referred to as "bank holidays" in the UK?
A) Religious holidays
B) Secular holidays
C) National holidays
D) Federal holidays

Q2. True or false? Diwali, often called the "Festival of Lights," is celebrated by Hindus and Sikhs over five days in October or November.

Q3. Which holiday is observed in Northern Ireland in July?
A) St. Patrick's Day
B) Remembrance Day
C) The anniversary of the Battle of the Boyne
D) Bonfire Night

Q4. Which public holiday involves fireworks and bonfires?
A) Christmas
B) Bonfire Night
C) St Patrick's Day
D) Bonfire Day

Q5. What is commonly eaten on Shrove Tuesday in the UK to celebrate the day before Lent?
A) Bacon and eggs
B) Fruit cake
C) Pancakes
D) Curry

Q6. In which country within the UK is the anniversary of the Battle of the Boyne observed as a public holiday?
A) England
B) Scotland
C) Wales
D) Northern Ireland

Q7. How do businesses typically respond to bank holidays?
A) They remain open as usual
B) They close for the day
C) They operate with reduced hours
D) They offer special promotions

Answers

Q1. What type of holidays are referred to as "bank holidays" in the UK?

Answer: B – Secular holidays

Note: Bank holidays do not hold religious significance and are primarily secular.

Q2. True or false? Diwali, often called the "Festival of Lights," is celebrated by Hindus and Sikhs over five days in October or November.

Answer: True

Q3. Which holiday is observed in Northern Ireland in July?

Answer: C – The anniversary of the Battle of the Boyne

Q4. Which public holiday involves fireworks and bonfires?

Answer: B – Bonfire Night

Q5. What is commonly eaten on Shrove Tuesday in the UK to celebrate the day before Lent?

Answer: C – Pancakes

Q6. In which country within the UK is the anniversary of the Battle of the Boyne observed as a public holiday?

Answer: D – Northern Ireland

Q7. How do businesses typically respond to bank holidays?

Answer: B – They close for the day

Sport

Sports are a vital part of life in the UK, deeply embedded in the culture. Many renowned sports, such as cricket, football, lawn tennis, golf, and rugby, originated in Britain.

Sports enthusiasts in the UK enjoy events held at prominent venues like Wembley Stadium in London and Millennium Stadium in Cardiff. Local governments and private enterprises offer a variety of sports facilities, including swimming pools, tennis courts, football pitches, dry ski slopes, and gyms.

The UK has hosted the Olympic Games three times: in 1908, 1948, and 2012, with the 2012 Games taking place in Stratford, East London. The British team excelled, securing third place in the overall medal standings. Additionally, London hosted the Paralympic Games in 2012, an event inspired by Dr. Sir Ludwig Guttmann, a German refugee. Guttmann, who worked at Stoke Mandeville Hospital in Buckinghamshire, pioneered rehabilitation methods for spinal injury patients and promoted sports as part of their recovery.

Notable British Sportsmen & Women

Sir Roger Bannister made history in 1954 by becoming the first person to run a mile in under four minutes.

Sir Jackie Stewart, a former Scottish racing driver, won the Formula 1 World Championship three times.

Bobby Moore captained the England football team to victory in the 1966 World Cup.

Sir Ian Botham, a former captain of the English cricket team, holds numerous records in both batting and bowling in English Test cricket.

Jayne Torvill and **Christopher Dean** won gold medals in ice dancing at the 1984 Olympics and secured four consecutive World Championship titles.

Sir Steve Redgrave is renowned for winning gold medals in rowing at five consecutive Olympic Games, establishing himself as one of Britain's greatest Olympians.

Baroness Tanni-Grey Thompson, a wheelchair athlete, earned 16 Paralympic medals, including 11 gold, over five Paralympic Games, and set 30 world records. She also won the London Marathon six times.

Dame Kelly Holmes secured two gold medals in running at the 2004 Olympics and set several British and European records.

Dame Ellen MacArthur set the record in 2004 for the fastest solo circumnavigation of the globe.

Sir Chris Hoy, a Scottish cyclist, achieved six gold and one silver Olympic medals, along with 11 world championship titles.

David Weir, a wheelchair Paralympian, won six gold medals over two Paralympic Games and claimed the London Marathon title six times.

Bradley Wiggins became the first Briton to win the Tour de France in 2012 and has won seven Olympic medals, including golds in 2004, 2008, and 2012.

Mo Farah, a British distance runner born in Somalia, won gold in the 5,000 and 10,000 metres at the 2012 Olympics, becoming the first Briton to win the 10,000 metres gold.

Jessica Ennis won the gold medal in the heptathlon at the 2012 Olympics, a multi-event track and field competition, and holds several British athletics records.

Andy Murray, a Scottish tennis player, won the US Open men's singles in 2012, becoming the first British man to win a Grand Slam singles title since 1936. He also won Olympic gold and silver medals and two-times winner of Wimbledon.

Ellie Simmonds, a Paralympic swimmer, won gold medals at the 2008 and 2012 Games and holds numerous world records. At the 2008 Games, she was the youngest member of the British team.

Cricket

Cricket, originating in England, has evolved into a global sport and is known for its distinctive and intricate rules. Matches can last up to five days and sometimes end in a draw, embodying the essence of British sportsmanship and fair play. The Ashes, a prestigious series of Test matches between England and Australia, is one of the most renowned cricket tournaments.

In the UK, cricket terminology often finds its way into everyday speech. For example:

- **"Rain stopped play"** indicates an unexpected interruption,
- **"Batting on a sticky wicket"** describes a challenging situation,
- **"Playing a straight bat"** means being honest and direct,
- **"Bowled a googly"** refers to an unexpected twist or surprise,
- **"It's just not cricket"** signifies behavior that is unfair or contrary to the spirit of the game.

Football

Football is the most popular sport in the UK, boasting a rich history that began in the late 19th century with the establishment of the first professional clubs. Each of the UK's four countries—England, Scotland, Wales, and Northern Ireland—has its own league system where clubs from various towns and cities compete.

The English Premier League stands out globally, attracting a massive international following and featuring many of the world's top players. UK teams also participate in European tournaments, including the UEFA Champions League. Fans are deeply invested in their local teams, often leading to fierce rivalries between clubs.

Each UK country has its own national team that competes in international tournaments such as the FIFA World Cup and the UEFA European Championships. England's sole international triumph came in the 1966 World Cup, which was held in the UK.

Football is also widely played at the grassroots level, with amateur matches taking place weekly in parks and fields throughout the UK.

Rugby

Rugby originated in England in the early 19th century and has since grown into a popular sport across the UK. There are two main types of rugby: rugby union and rugby league, each with its own set of rules and structure. Both forms feature distinct leagues and national teams in England, Wales, Scotland, and Northern Ireland (which compete with the Irish Republic).

The Six Nations Championship is the premier competition in rugby union, featuring teams from England, Ireland, Scotland, Wales, France, and Italy. In rugby league, the Super League is the most prominent club competition, showcasing top teams from the UK and beyond.

Horse-Racing

Horse racing in Britain boasts a deep historical legacy that extends back to the Roman era. The sport has longstanding connections with the royal family and features numerous racecourses throughout the country. Notable racing events include Royal Ascot, a prestigious five-day meeting in Berkshire attended by Royal Family members; the Grand National, held at Aintree near Liverpool; and the Scottish Grand National in Ayr. For those keen to explore the history of horse racing, the National Horseracing Museum in Newmarket, Suffolk, offers a comprehensive overview.

Golf

Golf originated in 15th-century Scotland and remains a popular sport in the UK, enjoyed both recreationally and professionally. The country is home to numerous public and private golf courses, with St Andrews in Scotland celebrated as the game's birthplace. The Open Championship, one of golf's major tournaments, is the only major held outside the United States and is hosted at a different course each year.

Tennis

Tennis originated in England in the late 19th century, with the first tennis club founded in Leamington Spa in 1872. Among the most renowned tennis events in the UK is The Wimbledon Championships, held each year at the All England Lawn Tennis and Croquet Club. As the oldest tennis tournament globally, Wimbledon is unique for being the only major event played on grass courts.

Water Sports

The UK's deep maritime heritage is evident in the ongoing enthusiasm for sailing. Numerous sailing events occur throughout the country, with the most prominent taking place in Cowes on the Isle of Wight. In 1966/67, Sir Francis Chichester became the first person to sail solo around the world, and two years later, Sir Robin Knox-Johnston achieved the first nonstop circumnavigation of the globe. Rowing is another favored activity and competitive sport, highlighted by the annual race on the Thames between Oxford and Cambridge Universities.

Motor Sports

Motor sports have a storied history in the UK, with car and motorcycle racing tracing back to 1902. The country continues to be a leader in motor-sport innovation and technology. It annually hosts a Formula 1 Grand Prix, and British drivers such as Damon Hill, Lewis Hamilton, and Jenson Button have all claimed the Formula 1 World Championship.

Skiing

Skiing is becoming increasingly popular in the UK, prompting many to travel abroad for skiing experiences. Dry ski slopes are spread across the country, and snow skiing is possible during the winter months. Scotland boasts five ski centres, and near Edinburgh is Europe's longest dry ski slope.

Revision Questions

Q1. Which country is credited with originating the game of cricket?

A) Australia

B) South Africa

C) England

D) India

Q2. What is the most famous cricket competition between England and Australia?

A) The Ashes

B) The World Cup

C) The Test Series

D) The Big Bash League

Q3. Which English football league is particularly known for attracting a global audience?

A) English Championship

B) National League

C) English Premier League

D) League One

Q4. Which major tennis tournament is held annually at the All England Lawn Tennis and Croquet Club?

A) The US Open

B) The French Open

C) The Australian Open

D) Wimbledon

Q5. Which of the following is the most famous rugby union competition?

A) The Super League

B) The Six Nations Championship

C) The Rugby World Cup

D) The Heineken Cup

Q6. What is the name of the annual rowing race between Oxford and Cambridge Universities?

A) The Boat Race

B) The Oxford-Cambridge Regatta

C) The Thames Challenge

D) The University Rowing Cup

Q7. Which British sailor became the first person to sail solo around the world in 1966/67?

A) Sir Robin Knox-Johnston

B) Sir Francis Chichester

C) Ellen MacArthur

D) Ben Ainslie

Q8. What significant event in horse racing is held annually at Aintree near Liverpool?

A) The Derby

B) The Grand National

C) The Oaks

D) The King George VI Chase

Q9. Where is Europe's longest dry ski slope located?

A) London

B) Manchester

C) Birmingham

D) Near Edinburgh

Q10. Which sport originated in Scotland in the 15th century and is still popular in the UK today?

A) Cricket

B) Golf

C) Tennis

D) Rugby

Answers

Q1. Which country is credited with originating the game of cricket?
Answer: C – England

Q2. What is the most famous cricket competition between England and Australia?
Answer: A – The Ashes

Q3. Which English football league is particularly known for attracting a global audience?
Answer: C – English Premier League

Q4. Which major tennis tournament is held annually at the All England Lawn Tennis and Croquet Club?
Answer: D – Wimbledon

Note: Wimbledon is the oldest tennis tournament in the world and is unique for its grass courts.

Q5. Which of the following is the most famous rugby union competition?
Answer: B – The Six Nations Championship

The Six Nations Championship features teams from England, Ireland, Scotland, Wales, France, and Italy.

Q6. What is the name of the annual rowing race between Oxford and Cambridge Universities?
Answer: A – The Boat Race

The Boat Race is a well-known annual event where Oxford and Cambridge compete on the Thames.

Q7. Which British sailor became the first person to sail solo around the world in 1966/67?
Answer: B – Sir Francis Chichester

Q8. What significant event in horse racing is held annually at Aintree near Liverpool?
Answer: B – The Grand National

Q9. Where is Europe's longest dry ski slope located?
Answer: D – Near Edinburgh

Q10. Which sport originated in Scotland in the 15th century and is still popular in the UK today?

Answer: B – Golf

Arts & Culture

Music

British music culture boasts a rich and diverse heritage, spanning from classical compositions to contemporary pop. The UK is home to a wide array of musical events and venues.

A major event in the classical music calendar is The Proms, an eight-week summer festival that has been held since 1927. Organised by the BBC, it features classical orchestral performances at venues including London's Royal Albert Hall, culminating in the celebrated Last Night of the Proms, which is broadcast nationwide.

Classical music has deep roots in the UK, with figures like Henry Purcell, who contributed a uniquely British style to church music and operas, and George Frideric Handel, a German-born British composer known for masterpieces such as *Water Music*, *Music for the Royal Fireworks*, and the oratorio *Messiah*. Notably, Handel's *Messiah* continues to be a staple in choral repertoires. The term "oratorio" refers to a large-scale musical composition for orchestra, choir, and soloists.

British classical music history also includes Gustav Holst, famed for *The Planets*, which inspired the hymn "I Vow to Thee, My Country"; Sir Edward Elgar, known for the *Pomp and Circumstance Marches*; Ralph Vaughan Williams, who infused his works with traditional English folk melodies; Sir William Walton, recognised for his film scores and operas; and Benjamin Britten, who composed influential operas like *Peter Grimes* and founded the Aldeburgh Festival.

In the realm of popular music, the UK has made a global impact with genres such as folk, jazz, pop, and rock. Iconic bands like The Beatles and The Rolling Stones have shaped the musical landscape both in the UK and internationally.

Major music venues like Wembley Stadium, The O2 in London, and the Scottish Exhibition and Conference Centre in Glasgow host numerous concerts and events throughout the year. Festivals such as Glastonbury, the Isle of Wight Festival, and V Festival showcase both established and emerging artists. Additionally, the National Eisteddfod of Wales celebrates Welsh music, dance, and poetry annually, while the Mercury Music Prize and Brit Awards recognise exceptional musical achievements in the UK and Ireland.

Theatre

The UK is home to a wide array of theatres, from small community spaces to grand venues, found in most towns and cities. These theatres play a crucial role in local culture, offering both professional and amateur productions. London's West End, often referred to as "Theatreland," is especially renowned. It is famous for long-running shows like *The Mousetrap*, a murder-mystery by Dame Agatha Christie, which has held the record for the longest-running show in history since it began in 1952.

The UK has a rich tradition in musical theatre. Gilbert and Sullivan's comic operas, such as *HMS Pinafore*, *The Pirates of Penzance*, and *The Mikado*, continue to be performed by both professionals and amateurs. Andrew Lloyd Webber's musicals, including *Jesus Christ Superstar*, *Evita*, *Cats*, and *The Phantom of the Opera*, are celebrated globally.

Pantomime is a distinctive British theatrical tradition, particularly popular during the Christmas season. These performances are based on fairy tales and are known for their music, comedy, and family-friendly content. Traditional pantomime characters include the Dame, a male actor in a female role, and a pantomime horse or cow, typically played by two actors in one costume.

The Edinburgh Festival, held every summer in Edinburgh, Scotland, is a prominent series of arts and cultural festivals. The Edinburgh Festival Fringe, the largest and most famous of these, features a diverse range of theatre and comedy, often showcasing experimental work.

The Laurence Olivier Awards, named after the esteemed British actor Sir Laurence Olivier, recognise excellence in theatre. These awards, presented annually in London, honor outstanding performances across various categories, including best director, actor, and actress. Sir Laurence Olivier was celebrated for his roles in numerous Shakespearean plays.

Art

During the Middle Ages, art predominantly featured religious themes, including wall paintings in churches and illustrations in religious manuscripts. After the Protestant Reformation, much of this religious art was lost. However, wealthy families began to acquire paintings and sculptures on a broader range of subjects. In the 16th and 17th centuries, many prominent artists working in Britain were from abroad, such as Hans Holbein and Sir Anthony Van Dyck. From the 18th century onwards, British artists, especially those specializing in portraits and landscapes, began to gain wider recognition.

Today, artworks by both British and international artists are displayed in galleries across the UK. Notable institutions include The National Gallery, Tate Britain, and Tate Modern in London; the National Museum in Cardiff; and the National Gallery of Scotland in Edinburgh.

The Turner Prize, established in 1984 and named after the artist Joseph Turner, celebrates contemporary art. Each year, four works are shortlisted and exhibited at Tate Britain before the winner is announced. This prestigious award is one of the most esteemed in Europe, with past winners including Damien Hirst and Richard Wright.

Notable British Artists

Thomas Gainsborough was a prominent portrait painter, celebrated for his depictions of individuals set against lush countryside or garden backgrounds.

David Allan, a Scottish artist, is best known for his portraits and his notable work, *The Origin of Painting*.

Joseph Turner revolutionised landscape painting with a modern approach that elevated the genre's status.

John Constable earned acclaim for his portrayals of Dedham Vale in eastern England, near the Suffolk-Essex border.

The Pre-Raphaelites, active in the latter half of the 19th century, were renowned for their vivid, detailed portrayals of religious and literary themes. Key members included Holman Hunt, Dante Gabriel Rossetti, and Sir John Millais.

Sir John Lavery, a distinguished Northern Irish portrait painter, included members of the Royal Family among his subjects.

Henry Moore, an English artist and sculptor, is widely recognised for his monumental abstract bronze sculptures.

John Petts, a Welsh artist, gained recognition for his engravings and stained glass works.

Lucian Freud, a German-born British artist, is renowned for his intense and detailed portraiture.

David Hockney was a leading figure in the 1960s pop art movement and continues to influence contemporary art significantly.

Architecture

The UK boasts a rich and varied architectural heritage. During the Middle Ages, the construction of impressive cathedrals and churches became prominent, with many still standing today, such as those in Durham, Lincoln, Canterbury, and Salisbury. The White Tower at the Tower of London, a quintessential Norman castle keep, was built under William the Conqueror's reign.

As times became more peaceful and landowners grew wealthier, the architecture of their country homes became more elaborate. Notable examples include Hardwick Hall in Derbyshire, which marks the beginning of a distinct British architectural evolution.

In the 17th century, Inigo Jones drew inspiration from classical architecture to design significant buildings like the Queen's House at Greenwich and the Banqueting House in Whitehall, London. Later, Sir Christopher Wren contributed to a uniquely British adaptation of the ornate European styles with landmarks such as the newly rebuilt St Paul's Cathedral.

The 18th century saw a shift towards simpler designs. Scottish architect Robert Adam had a considerable influence on British, European, and American architecture, designing interiors and structures like Dumfries House in Scotland. His work also impacted cities like Bath, exemplified by the Royal Crescent.

The 19th century witnessed a revival of medieval Gothic architecture. This style adorned numerous public buildings, including the Houses of Parliament and St Pancras Station, as well as town halls in Manchester and Sheffield.

In the 20th century, Sir Edwin Lutyens extended his architectural influence globally, designing New Delhi as India's administrative capital. Post-World War I, he created numerous war memorials, including the Cenotaph in Whitehall, which hosts the annual Remembrance Day service attended by the monarch, politicians, and foreign dignitaries.

Contemporary British architects such as Sir Norman Foster, Lord Richard Rogers, and Dame Zaha Hadid are renowned for their groundbreaking work both in the UK and internationally.

Garden design and landscaping also play a crucial role in British architecture. In the 18th century, Lancelot "Capability" Brown transformed country house grounds to appear naturally picturesque, often noting the "capabilities" of a location. Gertrude Jekyll later worked with Edwin Lutyens to create vibrant gardens around his architectural projects. Gardens remain a significant element of UK homes, with the Chelsea Flower Show showcasing garden design from both Britain and around the globe.

Fashion & Design

Britain has a rich history of outstanding designers. From Thomas Chippendale, known for his 18th-century furniture designs, to Clarice Cliff, celebrated for her Art Deco ceramics, and Sir Terence Conran, a leading interior designer of the 20th century, the country has produced remarkable talent. In the fashion world, recent decades have seen influential designers like Mary Quant, Alexander McQueen, and Vivienne Westwood making significant contributions.

Literature

The UK boasts a rich literary heritage, with a host of British writers having won the Nobel Prize in Literature, including the novelist Sir William Golding, poet Seamus Heaney, and playwright Harold Pinter. Beyond these laureates, many British authors have gained fame for their popular fiction. Agatha Christie's detective novels are read worldwide, while Ian Fleming's books introduced the legendary character of James Bond. In 2003, J.R.R. Tolkien's *The Lord of the Rings* was celebrated as the nation's favourite novel.

Since 1968, the Man Booker Prize for Fiction has been awarded annually to recognise outstanding novels by authors from the Commonwealth, Ireland, or Zimbabwe. Notable past winners include Ian McEwan, Hilary Mantel, and Julian Barnes.

Notable Authors & Writers

Jane Austen was an English novelist renowned for her insightful explorations of marriage and family in works such as *Pride and Prejudice* and *Sense and Sensibility*. Her novels have been widely adapted for television and film.

Charles Dickens, a prominent 19th-century English novelist, authored classics like *Oliver Twist* and *Great Expectations*. His memorable characters, including Scrooge and Mr. Micawber, have become entrenched in everyday language.

Robert Louis Stevenson is celebrated for his enduring works for both adults and children, including *Treasure Island*, *Kidnapped*, and *Strange Case of Dr Jekyll and Mr Hyde*.

Thomas Hardy, an influential author and poet, is known for his novels that delve into rural life, such as *Far from the Madding Crowd* and *Jude the Obscure*.

Sir Arthur Conan Doyle, a Scottish doctor and writer, gained fame for creating Sherlock Holmes, one of the earliest and most iconic fictional detectives.

Evelyn Waugh was a satirical novelist best known for works like *Brideshead Revisited*, as well as *Decline and Fall* and *Scoop*.

Sir Kingsley Amis was an English novelist and poet, with over 20 novels to his name, the most celebrated being *Lucky Jim*.

Graham Greene's novels often reflect his religious views, with notable works including *The Heart of the Matter*, *The Honorary Consul*, *Brighton Rock*, and *Our Man in Havana*.

J.K. Rowling is renowned for her globally successful *Harry Potter* series, which has captivated readers of all ages. She has also written fiction for adults.

British Poets

British poetry boasts a rich and storied tradition, beginning with the Anglo-Saxon epic *Beowulf*, which chronicles the hero's battles with mythical creatures. Medieval poetry includes Geoffrey Chaucer's *Canterbury Tales* and *Sir Gawain and the Green Knight*, a tale of one of King Arthur's knights. William Shakespeare, known for his plays, also penned numerous sonnets and longer poems, while John Milton's *Paradise Lost* reflects his religious beliefs.

Nature themes were prevalent among poets like William Wordsworth, while Sir Walter Scott drew inspiration from Scotland's folklore and traditions. The 19th century saw the emergence of influential poets such as William Blake, John Keats, Lord Byron, Percy Shelley, Alfred Lord Tennyson, and Robert and Elizabeth Browning.

In the 20th century, poets like Wilfred Owen and Siegfried Sassoon explored their World War I experiences, and more recent notable poets include Sir Walter de la Mare, John Masefield, Sir John Betjeman, and Ted Hughes. Many of these eminent poets are commemorated or buried in Poet's Corner at Westminster Abbey.

Revision Questions

Q1. Which epic poem from the Anglo-Saxon period tells the story of a hero battling mythical creatures?
A) *The Canterbury Tales*
B) *Sir Gawain and the Green Knight*
C) *Beowulf*
D) *Paradise Lost*

Q2. Which medieval poem features Geoffrey Chaucer's collection of stories told by pilgrims?
A) *Paradise Lost*
B) *Sir Gawain and the Green Knight*
C) *The Canterbury Tales*
D) *The Divine Comedy*

Q3. Which of the following works was written by William Shakespeare?
A) *Paradise Lost*
B) *The Canterbury Tales*
C) *The Raven*
D) *Sonnet 18*

Q4. Which of the following is an iconic British band of the 1960s?
A) One Direction
B) Savage Garden
C) The Beatles
D) The Spice Girls

Q5. Who was the renowned author of both *Pride and Prejudice* and *Sense and Sensibility*?
A) J.K. Rowling
B) Sir Walter Scott
C) John Keats
D) Jane Austin

Q6. The White Tower at the Tower of London, a quintessential Norman castle keep, was built under which leader's reign?
A) Boris Johnson
B) Queen Elizabeth II
C) William the Conqueror
D) Winston Churchill

Answers

Q1. Which epic poem from the Anglo-Saxon period tells the story of a hero battling mythical creatures?

Answer: C – *Beowulf*

Q2. Which medieval poem features Geoffrey Chaucer's collection of stories told by pilgrims?

Answer: C – The Canterbury Tales

Q3. Which of the following works was written by William Shakespeare?

Answer: D – *Sonnet 18*

Q4. Which of the following is an iconic British band of the 1960s?

Answer: C – The Beatles

Q5. Who was the renowned author of both *Pride and Prejudice* and *Sense and Sensibility*?

Answer: D – Jane Austin

Q6. The White Tower at the Tower of London, a quintessential Norman castle keep, was built under which leader's reign?

Answer: C – William the Conqueror

Leisure

People in the UK engage in a wide variety of leisure activities, reflecting their diverse interests and cultural traditions. In this section, we will explore how individuals across the country spend their free time, from participating in sports and attending cultural events to enjoying outdoor activities and exploring historical sites.

Whether it's through the excitement of attending a local football match, the enjoyment of a quiet afternoon at a historic garden, or the thrill of participating in traditional British events, leisure activities play a significant role in enhancing the quality of life and fostering community connections throughout the UK.

Gardening

The world of gardening in the UK is vibrant and diverse, ranging from grand national exhibitions to charming local shows. Garden centres are common in most towns, offering a wide selection of plants and gardening tools. The UK is home to some of the world's most celebrated gardens, including Kew Gardens, Sissinghurst, and Hidcote in England; Crathes Castle and Inveraray Castle in Scotland; Bodnant Garden in Wales; and Mount Stewart in Northern Ireland.

Gardens are a popular feature of many homes, where people often spend their leisure time tending to them. Additionally, many individuals rent plots of land, known as allotments, to grow fruits and vegetables. Each part of the UK has its own distinctive flowers, which are sometimes worn on national saints' days and hold special significance in local traditions.

Shopping

In the UK, shopping options are varied and plentiful. Most towns and cities feature a town centre that acts as the main shopping hub. Additionally, many shopping centres are situated either in or near these town centres, offering a wide range of retail experiences. While most shops are open daily, Sunday and public holiday hours may be reduced. Many towns also host regular markets, which occur weekly or more frequently, where vendors sell a diverse array of goods.

Cooking and Food

The UK has a rich cultural heritage and diverse population, resulting in a wide range of foods being enjoyed by its people. Cooking is a popular activity, with individuals frequently inviting one another over for dinner.

The UK has a variety of traditional foods that are commonly associated with different regions.

In England, one of the most iconic dishes is roast beef, which is typically served with potatoes, vegetables, Yorkshire puddings (batter that is baked in the oven), and other side dishes. Fish and chips are also popular.

In Wales, the traditional snack is Welsh cakes, made from flour, dried fruits, and spices, and served either hot or cold.

In Scotland, haggis is a well-known dish, consisting of a sheep's stomach stuffed with offal, suet, onions, and oatmeal.

In Northern Ireland, the Ulster fry is a hearty fried meal that includes bacon, eggs, sausage, black pudding, white pudding, tomatoes, mushrooms, soda bread, and potato bread.

Betting & Gambling

Gambling is a widely enjoyed pastime in the UK, with many people placing bets on sports and other events. Casinos are spread across various locations, offering additional opportunities for gaming. To access betting shops or gambling clubs, individuals must be at least 18 years old. Additionally, the National Lottery provides another popular gambling option, with weekly draws. While tickets and scratch cards are available for purchase, participation is restricted to those aged 16 and over.

Pets

In the UK, many people keep pets such as cats and dogs for companionship and enjoyment. Laws strictly prohibit cruelty or neglect towards animals. Dogs must wear a collar with the owner's name and address when in public. Owners are responsible for keeping their dogs under control and cleaning up after them in public spaces. Veterinary surgeons (vets) offer vaccinations and medical treatment for pets, and there are charities available to help those who may struggle to afford veterinary care for their animals.

Revision Questions

Q1. What is required for dogs when they are in public places in the UK?
A) They must be on a leash at all times
B) They must wear a collar with the owner's name and address
C) They must wear a muzzle
D) They must be accompanied by a veterinary certificate

Q2. What is prohibited by law regarding pets in the UK?
A) Pets must be exercised daily
B) Pets must be trained
C) Cruelty or neglect towards pets
D) Pets must be fed twice a day

Q3. What is the minimum age required to enter betting shops or gambling clubs in the UK?
A) 16 years old
B) 18 years old
C) 21 years old
D) 25 years old

Q4. Which of the following is not permitted for individuals under the age of 16 in the UK?
A) Purchasing lottery tickets
B) Buying scratch cards
C) Participating in the National Lottery
D) Entering gambling clubs

Q5. What can charities provide for pet owners in the UK?
A) Pet training programs
B) Financial assistance for veterinary care
C) Pet grooming services
D) Pet adoption services

Answers

Q1. What is required for dogs when they are in public places in the UK?

Answer: B – They must wear a collar with the owner's name and address

Q2. What is prohibited by law regarding pets in the UK?

Answer: C – Cruelty or neglect towards pets

Q3. What is the minimum age required to enter betting shops or gambling clubs in the UK?

Answer: B – 18 years old

Q4. Which of the following is not permitted for individuals under the age of 16 in the UK?

Answer: D – Entering gambling clubs

Q5. What can charities provide for pet owners in the UK?

Answer: B – Financial assistance for veterinary care

Films & Entertainment

British Film Industry

Modern cinema has been profoundly shaped by the UK, with public film screenings beginning in 1896. From its inception, British filmmakers have been celebrated for their innovative special effects, a tradition that continues to this day. Early British cinema stars like Sir Charles Chaplin achieved fame both in the UK and the USA, highlighting the UK's significant contribution to global cinema.

The 1930s saw British studios, including those led by notable directors such as Sir Alexander Korda and Sir Alfred Hitchcock, thrive. Films like *In Which We Serve* were instrumental in lifting morale during World War II. Subsequent decades saw British directors like Sir David Lean and Ridley Scott achieve international acclaim alongside their domestic successes.

British cinema also gained fame for its comedies in the 1950s and 1960s, with hits such as *Passport to Pimlico*, *The Ladykillers*, and the *Carry On* series capturing the public's imagination.

While many contemporary British films are produced by international companies utilizing UK talent, the country remains home to some of the most successful movie franchises ever, including *Harry Potter* and *James Bond*. The UK is also renowned for its excellence in animation, with Nick Park's *Wallace and Gromit* films earning four Oscars.

British actors have long made their mark on cinema, with legends such as Sir Laurence Olivier, David Niven, Sir Rex Harrison, and Richard Burton. Modern British stars like Colin Firth, Sir Anthony Hopkins, Dame Judi Dench, Kate Winslet, and Tilda Swinton continue to receive global recognition and awards.

The British Academy of Film and Television Arts (BAFTA) hosts the annual British Academy Film Awards, celebrating excellence in film and television as the UK's equivalent of the Oscars.

British Comedy

The UK boasts a rich tradition of comedy and satire, with self-deprecating humor being a cherished aspect of its national character. In medieval times, jesters entertained kings and nobles with jokes and courtly satire. Shakespeare also integrated comic characters into his plays, contributing to the country's comedic heritage.

By the 18th century, political cartoons began to flourish, mocking prominent politicians and sometimes even members of the royal family. The 19th century saw the rise of satirical magazines like *Punch*, which continues to this day alongside modern political cartoons and satirical publications such as *Private Eye*.

British music hall, a popular variety theatre form, featured comedians and became a major entertainment venue until television took the lead. Performers who started in the music halls, such as Morecambe and Wise, transitioned to television stardom in the 1940s and 1950s.

Television comedy has evolved with a distinctive style, with sitcoms focusing on family and workplace dynamics maintaining strong popularity. Satirical programs like *That Was The Week That Was* in the 1960s and *Spitting Image* in the 1980s and 1990s have played significant roles in British comedy. The 1969 debut of

Monty Python's Flying Circus introduced a groundbreaking form of progressive comedy. In recent years, stand-up comedy has enjoyed a resurgence, with solo comedians performing to live audiences.

Television & Radio

The UK offers a diverse range of television channels, with some available for free and others requiring a subscription. British TV features a variety of programmes, including popular soap operas such as *Coronation Street* and *EastEnders*. Regional programming is also prominent, with Scotland broadcasting in Gaelic, Wales offering a Welsh-language channel, and Northern Ireland providing both local content and programmes in Irish Gaelic.

A television licence is mandatory for anyone using a TV, computer, or other device to watch TV in the UK. This licence covers all equipment in a single household, although individuals in shared housing with separate tenancy agreements must each obtain their own licence. People over 75 can receive a free TV licence, and blind individuals are eligible for a 50% discount. Failure to obtain a licence can result in a fine of up to £1,000.

The British Broadcasting Corporation (BBC), funded by TV licence fees, is the world's largest broadcaster and the only fully state-funded media organisation that operates independently of government control. In contrast, other UK channels are financed through advertisements and subscriptions.

In addition to television, the UK boasts numerous radio stations. Some broadcast nationally, while others serve specific cities or regions. These stations offer a range of music and regional language programming, including Welsh and Gaelic. Like BBC television, BBC radio stations are funded by TV licence fees, whereas other radio stations rely on advertising for their revenue.

Social Networking

Social networking platforms such as Facebook, Instagram, WhatsApp, and Twitter have become key tools for people to keep in touch with friends, organise social gatherings, and share photos, videos, and opinions. Thanks to the accessibility of mobile devices, many users engage with these networks while on the move.

Pubs & Night Clubs

Pubs, or public houses, play a central role in UK social life, serving as popular spots for meeting friends and engaging in social activities. Most communities feature a local pub that acts as a hub for social gatherings. Pub quizzes are a common entertainment, and traditional games like pool and darts are frequently enjoyed.

In the UK, the legal drinking age is 18, so individuals must be at least this age to purchase alcohol in a pub or nightclub, although some pubs may permit minors if accompanied by an adult. At 16, individuals are allowed to drink wine or beer with a meal in a hotel, restaurant, or pub's dining area, provided they are accompanied by someone over 18.

Pubs generally open from 11:00 am (12 noon on Sundays), while nightclubs, which often feature dancing and music, usually operate later into the night. The pub or nightclub owner, known as the licensee, is responsible for determining the establishment's operating hours.

Revision Questions

Q1. What is a common activity at pubs in the UK?
A) Studying
B) Attending lectures
C) Playing traditional pub games
D) Watching movies

Q2. At what age can individuals in the UK legally purchase alcohol in a pub?
A) 16
B) 18
C) 21
D) 25

Q3. Can a 16-year-old drink alcohol in a pub if they are with an adult?
A) No
B) Yes, but only spirits
C) Yes, but only with a meal
D) Yes, with no restrictions

Answers

Q1. What is a common activity at pubs in the UK?

Answer: C – Playing traditional pub games

Q2. At what age can individuals in the UK legally purchase alcohol in a pub?

Answer: B – 18

Q3. Can a 16-year-old drink alcohol in a pub if they are with an adult?

Answer: C – Yes, but only with a meal.

Note: At 16, individuals can drink wine or beer with a meal if accompanied by someone over 18.

Places of Interest

The UK is home to a variety of iconic landmarks and natural wonders that showcase its rich history and diverse landscapes, including some of the following famous locations.

Big Ben, often used to refer to both the bell and the clock tower, is located at the Houses of Parliament in London. Although the clock tower was officially renamed the Elizabeth Tower in 2012 to honor Queen Elizabeth II's Diamond Jubilee, "Big Ben" remains a widely recognised name. The clock, more than 150 years old, is one of London's most visited attractions.

The Eden Project, located in Cornwall, England, features expansive biomes that mimic greenhouse environments to showcase plants from across the globe. It operates as a charity, promoting environmental sustainability and social initiatives worldwide.

Edinburgh Castle dominates the skyline of Edinburgh, Scotland. With origins dating back to the early Middle Ages, it is now managed by Historic Scotland, a government agency dedicated to preserving Scotland's historic sites.

The Giant's Causeway, found on Northern Ireland's northeast coast, is a striking geological formation composed of basalt columns formed by volcanic activity around 50 million years ago. Its unique structure is steeped in local legends and folklore.

Loch Lomond and the Trossachs National Park, covering 720 square miles (1,865 square kilometers) in western Scotland, is renowned for Loch Lomond, the largest freshwater lake in mainland Britain. The park offers breathtaking scenery and diverse wildlife.

The London Eye, a 443-foot (135-meter) tall Ferris wheel on the south bank of the River Thames, was constructed to mark the millennium. It continues to be a major attraction and a highlight of New Year's celebrations.

Snowdonia National Park, located in North Wales, spans over 838 square miles (2,170 square kilometers) and is renowned for its rugged terrain. Snowdon, the park's highest peak, is a prominent feature and popular destination for hikers.

The Tower of London, built by William the Conqueror in 1066, is a historic fortress and home to the Crown Jewels. It is guarded by Yeoman Warders, commonly known as Beefeaters, who provide informative tours of the site.

The Lake District, England's largest national park, covers 885 square miles (2,292 square kilometers) and is celebrated for its scenic lakes and mountains. Popular among climbers, walkers, and sailors, Windermere is the park's largest lake. In 2007, Wastwater was voted Britain's favorite view by television viewers.

Revision Questions

Q1. What is the name of the bell commonly referred to as "Big Ben" in London?
A) The Queen's Bell
B) The Elizabeth Bell
C) The Big Bell
D) The Clock Tower Bell

Q2. Which UK landmark is known for its biomes that house plants from around the world?
A) The Eden Project
B) Kew Gardens
C) The Royal Botanic Gardens
D) The Eden Gardens

Q3. Which castle dominates the skyline of Edinburgh, Scotland?
A) Stirling Castle
B) Eilean Donan Castle
C) Edinburgh Castle
D) Balmoral Castle

Q4. What natural feature is the Giant's Causeway in Northern Ireland known for?
A) A mountain range
B) Basalt columns
C) A volcanic crater
D) A glacial lake

Q5. Which of the following is the largest freshwater lake in mainland Britain?
A) Loch Ness
B) Loch Lomond
C) Windermere
D) Loch Awe

Q6. What is the London Eye primarily known for?
A) Its historical significance
B) Its role in New Year's celebrations
C) Its botanical gardens
D) Its medieval architecture

Q7. Which national park in Wales is known for its highest peak, Snowdon?

A) Brecon Beacons National Park

B) Snowdonia National Park

C) Pembrokeshire Coast National Park

D) Gower Peninsula

Q8. What historic building in London is known for housing the Crown Jewels?

A) The Tower of London

B) Buckingham Palace

C) Westminster Abbey

D) Hampton Court Palace

Q9. Which of the following landmarks is known for its scenic lakes and mountains and is the largest national park in England?

A) The Lake District

B) The Cotswolds

C) Peak District

D) New Forest

Q10. What was the original purpose of the London Eye when it was built?

A) To serve as an observation tower

B) To function as a public park

C) To celebrate the new millennium

D) To provide a venue for concerts

Answers

Q1. What is the name of the bell commonly referred to as "Big Ben" in London?

Answer: D – The Clock Tower Bell

Note: The name "Big Ben" actually refers to the Great Bell of the clock in the Elizabeth Tower.

Q2. Which UK landmark is known for its biomes that house plants from around the world?

Answer: A – The Eden Project

Q3. Which castle dominates the skyline of Edinburgh, Scotland?

Answer: C – Edinburgh Castle

Q4. What natural feature is the Giant's Causeway in Northern Ireland known for?

Answer: B – Basalt columns

Q5. Which of the following is the largest freshwater lake in mainland Britain?

Answer: B – Loch Lomond

Q6. What is the London Eye primarily known for?

Answer: B – Its role in New Year's celebrations

Q7. Which national park in Wales is known for its highest peak, Snowdon?

Answer: B – Snowdonia National Park

Q8. What historic building in London is known for housing the Crown Jewels?

Answer: A – The Tower of London

Q9. Which of the following landmarks is known for its scenic lakes and mountains and is the largest national park in England?

Answer: A – The Lake District

Q10. What was the original purpose of the London Eye when it was built?

Answer: C – To celebrate the new millennium

Note: The London Eye has also since become a major tourist attraction.

Chapter 5: The UK Government, the Law & Your Role

This chapter offers a comprehensive overview of the UK's governance structure. It details the monarch's role and powers within the government, the appointment processes for members of the two Houses of Parliament, and the specific responsibilities of key positions such as the Speaker and the Cabinet. Understanding your rights to vote and run for office is also covered. For those taking the citizenship test in Scotland, Wales, or Northern Ireland, special attention should be given to the functions of the devolved administrations.

The chapter also explains the UK's international involvement, including its membership in the Commonwealth, the European Union, and other organisations, highlighting the distinctions between these bodies and their member states. It also provides an overview of common laws, fundamental rights, policing, and the judicial system, including the various courts and the types of cases they address. Additionally, the chapter discusses practical matters such as taxation, driving regulations, and community engagement.

The Development of British Democracy

The UK functions as a parliamentary democracy, with the monarch acting as the head of state. This section explores the key institutions within this democratic framework and explains how individuals can engage in the democratic process.

Democracy allows the entire adult population to take part in decision-making, either directly through voting or indirectly by electing representatives to make decisions on their behalf.

In the early 19th century, Britain was not as democratic as it is today. Voting rights were limited to a small group of property-owning men over the age of 21. Over the 19th century, the electorate expanded significantly, and political parties began to include ordinary citizens.

The Chartists, a reformist group from the 1830s and 1840s, advocated for significant changes, including universal male suffrage and equal representation. While their initial efforts seemed unsuccessful, many of their proposed reforms were adopted by 1918. Women gained the right to vote at 30 in 1918, and this was equalised with men at 21 in 1928. The voting age was further lowered to 18 for both men and women in 1969.

The British Constitution

A constitution outlines the fundamental principles and structures by which a country is governed, including the institutions that manage the country and the mechanisms to limit their power. Unlike many other nations, the British constitution is not contained in a single written document, leading to it being described as "unwritten." Instead, it has evolved over centuries through a combination of statutes, conventions, and established practices. While some advocate for a written constitution to enhance clarity and accountability, others argue that the flexibility of an unwritten constitution allows for more adaptive and effective governance.

Constitutional Institutions

The UK government is structured into several key branches, including:

- **The Monarchy**
- **Parliament**, which is divided into the House of Commons and the House of Lords
- **The Prime Minister**
- **The Cabinet**
- **The Judiciary** (also known as "the courts")
- **The Police**
- **The Civil Service**
- **Local Government**

In addition to the central government, Scotland, Wales, and Northern Ireland each have their own devolved governments with the authority to legislate on certain issues.

The Monarchy

The UK operates under a constitutional monarchy, where the monarch does not govern directly but appoints a government elected by the people. The king or queen invites the leader of the party with the most Members of Parliament (MPs) or a coalition leader to become the Prime Minister. While the monarch meets regularly with the Prime Minister to offer advice and support, the Prime Minister and Cabinet are responsible for making policy decisions.

The monarch plays important ceremonial roles, such as opening each new parliamentary session and delivering a speech outlining government policies for the coming year. All Acts of Parliament are enacted in the monarch's name. Additionally, the monarch represents the UK internationally by receiving foreign ambassadors, hosting visiting heads of state, and undertaking state visits to strengthen diplomatic and economic ties with other nations.

Serving as a symbol of stability and continuity, the monarch remains a consistent figurehead amid changes in government and Prime Ministers. They also help foster national identity and pride, as seen in the celebrations of Queen Elizabeth II's Diamond Jubilee and Platinum Jubilee.

The current monarch is King Charles III, who succeeded his mother, Queen Elizabeth II. Queen Elizabeth II, the longest-reigning monarch in British history, reigned from 1952 to 2022 and celebrated her Platinum Jubilee in 2022, marking 70 years on the throne. She was married to Prince Philip, Duke of Edinburgh.

The National Anthem

The current National Anthem of the UK is *God Save the King*. It is played at important national occasions and at events attended by the King or the Royal Family. The first verse is:

'God save our gracious King!

Long live our noble King!

God save the King!

Send his victorious,

Happy and glorious,

Long to reign over us,

God save the King!'

New citizens also swear or affirm loyalty to the King as part of the citizenship ceremony.

Oath of Allegiance

"I (name) swear by Almighty God that on becoming a British citizen, I will be faithful and bear true allegiance to His Majesty King Charles the Third, his Heirs and Successors, according to law."

System of Government

The UK functions as a parliamentary democracy. The country is divided into parliamentary constituencies, and during a General Election, voters in each constituency elect a representative known as a Member of Parliament (MP). These elected MPs collectively make up the House of Commons. The political party with the most MPs typically forms the government. If no single party wins a majority, a coalition government may be formed by two or more parties.

The House of Commons

The House of Commons is the more influential of the two parliamentary chambers due to its members being elected democratically. The Prime Minister and most cabinet members are drawn from the House of Commons, where they serve as Members of Parliament (MPs). Each MP represents a specific parliamentary constituency, which is a defined region within the country.

MPs have a range of responsibilities, including:

- Representing the interests and concerns of their constituency.
- Contributing to the development of new legislation.
- Overseeing and scrutinizing government actions.
- Participating in discussions on important national issues.

The House of Lords

Members of the House of Lords, often referred to as peers, are not elected and do not represent specific constituencies. The House of Lords has seen several changes in its role and composition over the past fifty years.

Before 1958, the House of Lords consisted primarily of:

1. Hereditary peers who inherited their titles.
2. Senior judges.
3. Bishops from the Church of England.

Since 1958, the Prime Minister has had the authority to nominate life peers, who hold their titles for life. Life peers are usually individuals with distinguished careers in politics, business, law, or other fields. These appointments are made by the monarch on the Prime Minister's recommendation and can also include nominations from other major political party leaders or suggestions from an independent Appointments Commission for non-party peers.

Since 1999, hereditary peers no longer automatically have the right to sit in the House of Lords. Instead, they elect a limited number of representatives to attend.

The House of Lords operates with a degree of independence from the government. It can propose amendments and new laws, which are then reviewed by the House of Commons. The House of Lords also reviews legislation passed by the House of Commons to ensure its effectiveness and holds the government accountable for its actions. Peers with specialised knowledge contribute valuable expertise to the legislative process. While the House of Commons can override decisions made by the House of Lords, such overrides are relatively rare.

The Speaker

The Speaker of the House of Commons is responsible for overseeing debates within the chamber and is the highest-ranking official in the House. Although the Speaker is an elected Member of Parliament (MP) representing a specific constituency, they must remain impartial and not affiliate with any political party. The Speaker is elected by fellow MPs through a secret ballot.

The primary role of the Speaker is to maintain order and ensure that debates follow parliamentary rules. This involves managing the time allocated for discussions, including ensuring that opposition members have their fair share of time to speak on various issues. Additionally, the Speaker represents Parliament during ceremonial events. Despite their impartial role, the Speaker still addresses constituents' concerns and advocates on their behalf.

Elections

Members of Parliament (MPs) are elected during General Elections, which are held at least every five years. If an MP dies or resigns, a by-election is conducted in their constituency to fill the vacant seat.

Elections for MPs use the "first past the post" system, where the candidate with the most votes in each constituency is elected. The party that wins the most constituencies typically forms the government. If no single party gains a majority, a coalition government may be formed by two or more parties.

European Parliamentary elections occur every five years as well. In these elections, representatives known as Members of the European Parliament (MEPs) are chosen using proportional representation. This system allocates seats to parties in proportion to the number of votes they receive.

Contacting Elected Members

Elected representatives are tasked with serving and representing their constituents. You can find contact information for your representatives and their parties at your local library or on the official website, www.parliament.uk. Directories such as The

Phone Book by BT and Yellow Pages also list the contact details of MPs, Assembly members, Members of the Scottish Parliament (MSPs), and MEPs.

To contact an MP, you can write a letter or call their constituency office or their office in the House of Commons.

Many MPs, Assembly members, MSPs, and MEPs hold regular local "surgeries" where constituents can meet them in person to discuss issues. Details about these surgeries are usually advertised in local newspapers.

Revision Questions

Q1. What is the primary role of an MP (Member of Parliament)?

A) To manage local councils

B) To serve and represent their constituents

C) To appoint judges

D) To oversee local businesses

Q2. How often are General Elections held in the UK?

A) Every year

B) Every 2 years

C) Every 5 years

D) Every 10 years

Q3. What system is used to elect MPs in the UK?

A) Proportional representation

B) Mixed-member proportional

C) First past the post

D) Single transferable vote

Q4. Where can you find contact information for your MP?

A) Only in local newspapers

B) At your local library and www.parliament.uk

C) Only through personal visits

D) Through social media only

Q5. What is the address of the House of Commons?

A) 10 Downing Street, London

B) The Royal Exchange, London

C) The House of Lords, Westminster

D) The Palace of Westminster, London

Q6. What happens if an MP dies or resigns before the end of their term?

A) A new General Election is held

B) A by-election is held in their constituency

C) The Prime Minister appoints a replacement

D) The seat remains vacant until the next election

Q7. How are Members of the European Parliament (MEPs) elected?

A) Through a direct vote in each constituency

B) Using the proportional representation system

C) Appointed by national governments

D) Nominated by political parties

Q8. How can constituents usually meet their MPs in person?

A) During a regular "surgery" held by the MP

B) At a local council meeting

C) At their party headquarters

D) During a national conference

Q9. What is the role of the Speaker of the House of Commons?

A) To create new laws

B) To maintain order during debates

C) To represent the UK internationally

D) To appoint new MPs

Q10. True or false? Members of Parliament are elected during General Elections, which are held at least every five years.

Answers

Q1. What is the primary role of an MP (Member of Parliament)?
Answer: B – To serve and represent their constituents

Q2. How often are General Elections held in the UK?
Answer: C – Every 5 years

Q3. What system is used to elect MPs in the UK?
Answer: C – First past the post

Note: This system elects the candidate with the highest number of votes in each constituency.

Q4. Where can you find contact information for your MP?
Answer: B – At your local library and www.parliament.uk

Q5. What is the address of the House of Commons?
Answer: D – The Palace of Westminster, London

Q6. What happens if an MP dies or resigns before the end of their term?
Answer: B – A by-election is held in their constituency

Q7. How are Members of the European Parliament (MEPs) elected?
Answer: B – Using the proportional representation system

Q8. How can constituents usually meet their MPs in person?
Answer: A – During a regular "surgery" held by the MP
Note: "Surgeries" are local meetings where constituents can discuss issues with their MP.

Q9. What is the role of the Speaker of the House of Commons?
Answer: B – To maintain order during debates
Note: The Speaker ensures that parliamentary debates follow rules and are conducted fairly.

Q10. True or false? Members of Parliament are elected during General Elections, which are held at least every five years.
Answer: True

The Government

The Prime Minister

The Prime Minister (PM) is the leader of the ruling political party and wields considerable power within the UK government. They are responsible for appointing cabinet members and influencing key public appointments. The Prime Minister's official residence is 10 Downing Street, located in central London near the Houses of Parliament. They also have a country residence called Chequers, situated outside London. The position of Prime Minister can change if the governing party decides to replace them or if the Prime Minister resigns, often following a defeat in a General Election.

The Cabinet

The Prime Minister has the power to appoint around 20 senior Members of Parliament to lead various government departments. Key ministerial positions include:

- **Chancellor of the Exchequer**: Manages the economy and financial matters.
- **Home Secretary**: Oversees crime, policing, and immigration.
- **Foreign Secretary**: Handles diplomatic relations with other countries.
- **Secretaries of State**: Lead departments focused on areas such as education, health, and defense.

These ministers form the cabinet, a key committee that meets regularly to discuss and make major decisions on government policies. Such decisions often require debate and approval from Parliament. In addition to these senior ministers, each department includes other roles such as Ministers of State and Parliamentary Under-Secretaries of State, who manage specific functions within their departments.

The Opposition

The opposition party in the House of Commons is the second-largest party and is poised to lead if it wins the next General Election. The leader of the opposition has a critical role in scrutinizing and critiquing the government's actions and policies. A key platform for this is Prime Minister's Questions, held weekly during Parliament sessions, where the leader can question and challenge the Prime Minister. Additionally, the leader of the opposition appoints senior members from their party as "shadow ministers," who form the shadow cabinet. This shadow cabinet's role is to challenge government policies and propose alternative solutions.

The Party System

To stand as a candidate for Member of Parliament (MP), an individual must be at least 18 years old. While any eligible person can run, candidates endorsed by major political parties, such as the Conservative Party, the Labour Party, the Liberal Democrats, or regional parties from Scotland, Wales, or Northern Ireland, generally have a higher chance of winning.

Though most MPs are affiliated with these main parties, some are "independents," running without party backing and often focusing on issues important to their constituencies.

Major political parties encourage public involvement by inviting people to engage in debates, contribute financially, and assist during elections. They maintain local branches in many constituencies and hold annual conferences to shape their policies.

Pressure groups and lobbying organisations also play a significant role in shaping government policies. These include sector-specific groups like the Confederation of British Industry (CBI) for businesses, as well as advocacy groups such as Greenpeace for environmental issues and Liberty for human rights.

The Civil Service

Civil servants are essential in helping the government develop and implement policies and deliver crucial public services. They are appointed based on merit, ensuring they remain politically neutral and are not influenced by political affiliations. Those interested in joining the civil service can apply through a standardised application process, similar to other job applications in the UK.

Civil servants are expected to demonstrate high levels of dedication and commitment to their roles, adhering to the core values of the civil service. These values—integrity, honesty, objectivity, and impartiality—ensure that civil servants maintain professional standards and operate without political bias.

Local Government

Towns, cities, and rural areas across the UK are governed by democratically elected councils, known as "local authorities." In some regions, separate district and county councils handle different responsibilities, while larger towns and cities typically have a single local authority managing governance.

Local authorities are essential for providing a range of services within their areas and are funded through a mix of central government grants and local taxes.

Many local authorities appoint a mayor as a ceremonial leader, while in some towns, an elected mayor takes on a more active role in administration. In London, governance is managed by 33 local authorities, with the Greater London Authority and the Mayor of London overseeing policy coordination across the capital. Local elections for councillors are usually held annually in May, with many candidates running as representatives of political parties.

Devolved Administrations

Since 1997, the UK government has devolved certain powers to Wales, Scotland, and Northern Ireland to allow these regions greater autonomy in handling local matters. The Welsh Assembly and Scottish Parliament were established in 1999, and Northern Ireland has its own Assembly, which has had periods of suspension.

While key policy areas such as defence, foreign affairs, immigration, taxation, and social security remain under the central UK government's control, other public services, including education, are managed by the devolved administrations.

Each of these devolved administrations operates its own civil service.

The Welsh Government

The Welsh Government and the National Assembly for Wales are based in Cardiff, the capital city of Wales. The National Assembly comprises 60 Assembly Members (AMs), who are elected every four years using a proportional representation system. AMs can communicate in both Welsh and English, and all Assembly publications are available in both languages.

The Assembly has legislative authority over 20 areas, including education, health and social services, economic development, and housing. Since 2011, the National Assembly for Wales has had the power to enact legislation in these areas independently of the UK Parliament.

The Scottish Parliament

Founded in 1999, the Scottish Parliament meets in Edinburgh, the capital of Scotland. It is made up of 129 Members of the Scottish Parliament (MSPs), who are elected through a proportional representation system. The Scottish Parliament has the authority to legislate on all issues not specifically reserved to the UK Parliament. Its areas of jurisdiction include civil and criminal law, health, education, planning, and certain tax-raising powers.

The Northern Ireland Assembly

Established under the Belfast Agreement (Good Friday Agreement) in 1998, the Northern Ireland Assembly operates with a power-sharing arrangement that allocates ministerial positions among the main political parties. The Assembly consists of 108 elected Members of the Legislative Assembly (MLAs), chosen through proportional representation.

The Assembly is responsible for making decisions on various matters including education, agriculture, the environment, health, and social services. While the UK government retains the authority to suspend the devolved assemblies if necessary, this power has been exercised in Northern Ireland during periods of political instability. The Northern Irish Assembly has been suspended twice in recent years (2017-2020 and 2022-2024).

The Media & Government

Parliamentary proceedings are both televised and recorded in official reports known as Hansard. These records are available in major libraries and can also be accessed online at www.parliament.uk. Many people rely on newspapers (often called "the press"), television, radio, and the Internet as their primary sources for political news and events.

The UK values a free press, meaning newspapers operate independently from government influence. Owners and editors of newspapers may have strong political views and can use their platforms to campaign and sway public opinion or government policies.

Legally, radio and television must provide fair and balanced coverage of political parties, ensuring that all viewpoints receive equal time. This regulation helps maintain a level playing field for diverse political perspectives.

Who Can Vote?

The UK has operated under a fully democratic voting system since 1928. The voting age was lowered to 18 in 1969, and, with a few exceptions, all UK-born and naturalised adult citizens are entitled to vote.

In addition to UK citizens, adults from the Commonwealth and the Irish Republic who reside in the UK can vote in all public elections. However, citizens of other EU countries living in the UK can vote in most elections, except for General Elections.

The Electoral Register

To vote in parliamentary, local, or European elections, your name must be on the electoral register.

If you are eligible, you can register by contacting your local council's electoral registration office, which is usually located at your local council office (or elsewhere in Scotland). To find out which local authority covers your area, visit www.aboutmyvote.co.uk and enter your postcode. Voter registration forms are available in English, Welsh, and several other languages.

The electoral register is updated annually in September or October. Each household receives an electoral registration form that must be completed and returned, listing all residents who are eligible to vote.

In Northern Ireland, the process is different and involves "individual registration." Each eligible voter must fill out their own registration form. Once registered, you remain on the register as long as your details stay the same. For more information, visit the Electoral Office for Northern Ireland's website at www.eoni.org.uk.

By law, each local authority must make its electoral register available for public viewing, though it must be supervised. The register is held at local electoral registration offices (or council offices in England and Wales) and can also be viewed at certain public buildings like libraries.

Where to Vote

In elections, you cast your vote at designated polling stations (or polling places in Scotland). Before the election, you'll receive a poll card detailing the location of your polling station or place and the election date. On election day, polling stations or places are open from 7:00 am to 10:00 pm.

When you arrive at the polling station, staff will ask for your name and address. In Northern Ireland, you'll also need to provide photographic identification. You will then be given a ballot paper, which you take to a polling booth to complete in private. You should make your own decision on who to vote for; no one can influence your choice. Follow the instructions on the ballot paper, and after filling it out, place it in the ballot box.

If getting to a polling station is challenging, you can apply for a postal ballot. Your ballot paper will be sent to your home before the election. You fill it out and mail it back. You can request a postal ballot when you register to vote.

Standing for Office

Most UK citizens, as well as those from the Irish Republic or the Commonwealth, who are 18 or older, can run for public office. However, there are exceptions, including:

- Members of the armed forces
- Civil servants
- Individuals convicted of certain criminal offences

Members of the House of Lords are not eligible to stand for election to the House of Commons but can seek other public offices.

Visiting Parliament & the Devolved Administrations

Members of the public can attend and observe debates in both the House of Commons and the House of Lords at the Palace of Westminster. Public galleries are available for this purpose.

To obtain tickets, you can either write in advance to your local Member of Parliament or queue at the public entrance on the day of your visit. Entrance is free, but be prepared for potentially long wait times of one to two hours for the House of Commons. Access to the House of Lords is generally easier.

For more information, visit the UK Parliament website at www.parliament.uk.

Northern Ireland Assembly

In Northern Ireland, elected members known as MLAs meet at Stormont in Belfast for the Northern Ireland Assembly. To arrange a visit, you can either contact the Education Service (details available on the Northern Ireland Assembly website or reach out to an MLA.

Scottish Parliament

In Scotland, elected members, or MSPs, hold meetings at the Scottish Parliament building in Holyrood, Edinburgh. Visitor services can assist with information, ticket bookings, and tour arrangements.

National Assembly for Wales

In Wales, elected members, known as AMs, gather at the Welsh Assembly in the Senedd, Cardiff Bay. The Senedd offers guided tours and public gallery seating, which can be booked through the Assembly Booking Service.

Revision Questions

Q1. Where can members of the public attend and listen to debates in the UK Parliament?

A) The Queen's House

B) The Palace of Westminster

C) The Royal Court

D) Buckingham Palace

Q2. What is the general procedure for obtaining tickets to attend a debate in the House of Commons?

A) Purchase tickets online

B) Write to your local MP or queue at the entrance

C) Apply through a lottery system

D) Reserve through a travel agency

Q3. Which of the following is not a key ministerial position in the UK Cabinet?

A) Home Secretary

B) Foreign Secretary

C) Chancellor of the Exchequer

D) Minister of Sport

Q4. True or false? To stand as a candidate for Member of Parliament (MP), an individual must be at least 17 years old.

Q5. What is the name of the building where the Scottish Parliament meets?

A) Holyrood Palace

B) The Scottish Hall

C) The Parliament House

D) The Scottish Parliament building

Q6. Which assembly meets at the Senedd in Cardiff Bay?

A) The Welsh Assembly

B) The Welsh Parliament

C) The National Assembly for Wales

D) The Cardiff Assembly

Answers

Q1. Where can members of the public attend and listen to debates in the UK Parliament?

Answer: B – The Palace of Westminster

Q2. What is the general procedure for obtaining tickets to attend a debate in the House of Commons?

Answer: B – Write to your local MP or queue at the entrance

Q3. Which of the following is not a key ministerial position in the UK Cabinet?

Answer: D – Minister of Sport

Q4. True or false? To stand as a candidate for Member of Parliament (MP), an individual must be at least 17 years old.

Answer: False

An individual must be at least 18 years old to stand as a candidate for Member of Parliament.

Q5. What is the name of the building where the Scottish Parliament meets?

Answer: D – The Scottish Parliament building

The building is located in Holyrood, Edinburgh.

Q6. Which assembly meets at the Senedd in Cardiff Bay?

Answer: C – The National Assembly for Wales

The UK & International Institutions

The Commonwealth

The Commonwealth is an association of nations that work together to support common goals in democracy and progress. The organisation is founded on key principles of democracy, good governance, and the rule of law.

While many of its member states have historical connections to the former British Empire, some countries that were never colonies have also joined the union.

The King serves as the symbolic head of the Commonwealth, which currently includes 56 member states. Membership is voluntary, and although the Commonwealth does not have authority over its members, it can suspend membership if necessary.

The European Union

The European Union (EU), originally called the European Economic Community (EEC), was created by the Treaty of Rome, signed on 25 March 1957 by six Western European countries: Belgium, France, Germany, Italy, Luxembourg, and the Netherlands. Although the United Kingdom initially opted out, it joined the EU in 1973. The UK remained a member for nearly five decades before voting to leave the union in a 2016 referendum, a decision commonly referred to as "Brexit." After prolonged negotiations, the UK officially exited the EU on 31 January 2020, marking a historic shift in the political and economic landscape of Europe.

The Council of Europe

The Council of Europe operates separately from the European Union and consists of 47 member countries, including the United Kingdom. Its main focus is to protect and promote human rights across its member states. While it does not have legislative power, the Council develops conventions and charters, with the most notable being the European Convention on Human Rights.

The United Nations

The United Kingdom is a member of the United Nations (UN), an international organisation with over 190 member countries. Established after World War II, the UN aims to prevent conflicts and promote global peace and security. The Security Council, a key component of the UN, has 15 members responsible for recommending actions in response to international crises and threats. The UK holds one of the five permanent seats on the Security Council, giving it a crucial role in global decision-making.

The North Atlantic Treaty Organisation (NATO)

The United Kingdom is a member of NATO, a coalition of countries from Europe and North America. NATO is based on the principle of collective defense, where member nations commit to support one another if attacked. The alliance also aims to maintain peace among its members.

Revision Questions

Q1. How many countries are currently included in the Commonwealth?
A) 50
B) 100
C) 45
D) 56

Q2. True or false? The UK is no longer a member of the North Atlantic Treaty Organisation (NATO).

Q3. True or false? The Council of Europe does not have legislative power.

Q4. In which year did the UK officially exit the European Union?
A) 1973
B) 2020
C) 2016
D) 2011

Answers

Q1. How many countries are currently included in the Commonwealth?
A) 50
B) 100
C) 45
D) 56
Answer: D – 56

Q2. True or false? The UK is no longer a member of the North Atlantic Treaty Organisation (NATO).
Answer: False

Q3. True or false? The Council of Europe does not have legislative power.
Answer: True

Q4. In which year did the UK officially exit the European Union?
Answer: B – 2020

The Law in the UK

Understanding and following the law is a crucial responsibility for everyone living in the UK. This section offers an overview of the UK's legal system and highlights some laws that may affect you. While the UK is known for its inclusivity, all residents, regardless of their backgrounds, must adhere to local laws. Actions that are legal elsewhere might not be acceptable in the UK, and those who ignore the law should not expect to secure permanent residency.

Law impacts every aspect of life in the UK. It is important to be aware of the laws that influence your daily activities, both personal and professional. Staying informed about your legal obligations will help you comply with the law and manage your responsibilities effectively.

Respecting the Law

Equal treatment under the law is a core principle in the UK, ensuring that everyone is held to the same legal standards regardless of their background or origin. UK laws are generally divided into two main categories: criminal law and civil law.

Criminal Law deals with offences that are investigated by the police or relevant authorities and punished by the courts. Examples of criminal offences include:

1. **Carrying a weapon:** Possessing any weapon, including guns, knives, or items designed or adapted to cause harm, is illegal, even if intended for self-defense.
2. **Drugs:** The sale or purchase of illegal drugs such as heroin, cocaine, ecstasy, and cannabis is prohibited.
3. **Racial crime:** Harassing, alarming, or distressing someone based on their religion or ethnicity is a criminal offence.
4. **Selling tobacco:** Selling tobacco products like cigarettes or roll-up tobacco to those under 18 is illegal.
5. **Smoking in public places:** Most enclosed public areas in the UK are designated no-smoking zones, marked by appropriate signage.
6. **Buying alcohol:** It is illegal to sell alcohol to individuals under 18 or to buy alcohol on their behalf, though those aged 16 or over can consume it with a meal in a hotel or restaurant.
7. **Drinking in public:** Some areas have alcohol-free zones where drinking in public is banned. The police can confiscate alcohol and disperse individuals, with potential fines or arrests.

This list is not exhaustive; other serious crimes such as murder, theft, and assault are also included in criminal law.

Civil Law addresses disputes between individuals or groups and covers various areas, such as:

1. **Housing law:** Resolves issues between landlords and tenants, including disputes over repairs and evictions.
2. **Consumer rights:** Deals with disputes related to faulty goods or services.
3. **Employment law:** Handles cases involving wage disputes, unfair dismissal, or workplace discrimination.
4. **Debt:** Legal actions may be taken against individuals who owe money to others.

These examples illustrate some aspects of civil law, which covers a broad range of other legal issues as well.

The Police & Their Duties

The role of the police in the UK includes several key responsibilities:

- **Protecting lives and property**
- **Maintaining public order and preventing disturbances**
- **Preventing and investigating criminal activities**

UK police forces are structured as separate entities, each led by a Chief Constable, and operate independently of the government.

Since November 2012, Police and Crime Commissioners (PCCs) have been elected by the public in England and Wales. PCCs oversee the effective operation of the police force in their areas, setting local priorities and managing the local policing budget. They also have the authority to appoint the Chief Constable.

As a public service, the police are committed to assisting and protecting everyone, regardless of their background or residence. Police officers must adhere to strict codes of conduct and are prohibited from misusing their authority, making false statements, behaving rudely or abusively, or engaging in racial discrimination. Officers found guilty of corruption or misconduct face serious repercussions.

Supporting police officers are Police Community Support Officers (PCSOs), who have various duties depending on their area. Typically, PCSOs patrol neighbourhoods, engage with the public, and assist police officers at crime scenes and major events.

Individuals in the UK are expected to help the police in preventing and solving crimes. If someone is arrested and taken to a police station, they will be informed of the reason for their arrest and have the right to seek legal advice.

For addressing misconduct or grievances, there is a police complaints system. Complaints can be made at a police station or by writing to the Chief Constable of the relevant force. Additionally, complaints can be submitted to independent bodies such as the Independent Police Complaints Commission (England and Wales), the Police Complaints Commissioner (Scotland), or the Police Ombudsman (Northern Ireland).

Terrorism & Extremism

The UK faces a variety of terrorist threats, with the most notable coming from Al Qa'ida, its affiliated groups, and similar organisations. The country also contends with terrorism linked to other sources, including those related to Northern Ireland.

Terrorist groups use various tactics to radicalise and recruit individuals to advance their agendas. The methods and scope of these efforts can differ, but these groups usually receive limited public support. It is important for anyone wishing to live in the UK to be aware of these threats. Protecting all citizens involves combating different forms of extremism, such as opposition to core British values, religious extremism, and far-right extremism.

If you suspect someone is trying to recruit you to an extremist or terrorist cause, it is crucial to report this to your local police. This helps in maintaining public safety and preventing extremist activities.

Revision Questions

Q1. Which of the following is not an example of a criminal law offence?
A) Carrying a weapon
B) Racial crime
C) Illegal drug trade
D) Debt dispute

Q2. Which of the following is not an example of a civil law offence?
A) Debt dispute
B) Employment law dispute
C) Carrying a weapon
D) Housing law dispute

Q3. What should you do if you suspect someone is trying to recruit you to an extremist cause?
A) Ignore the situation
B) Seek legal advice
C) Inform your local police force
D) Discuss it with friends

Q4. Which independent bodies might handle complaints related to police conduct in the UK?
A) Local councils
B) Independent Police Complaints Commission
C) National government departments
D) International organisations

Answers

Q1. **Which of the following is not an example of a criminal law offence?**

Answer: D – Debt dispute

In the UK, debt disputes are treated as a civil law offence.

Q2. **Which of the following is not an example of a civil law offence?**

Answer: C – Carrying a weapon

In the UK, carrying a weapon is treated as a criminal law offence.

Q3. What should you do if you suspect someone is trying to recruit you to an extremist cause?

Answer: C – Inform your local police force

Reporting suspicions to the police helps in maintaining public safety and countering extremist activities.

Q4. Which independent bodies might handle complaints related to police conduct in the UK?

D) International organisations

Answer: B – Independent Police Complaints Commission

The Role of the Courts

The Judiciary

The judiciary, comprising a collective body of judges, plays a crucial role in interpreting the law and ensuring fair trials. It is essential to understand that the government is not permitted to interfere with this judicial process.

Occasionally, issues arise concerning the legality of government actions. If judges find such actions unlawful, the government must either revise its policies or pursue legislative changes through Parliament. When judges find that a public body is not upholding an individual's legal rights, they can order changes to practices and/or award compensation. Furthermore, judges resolve disputes between individuals or organisations, which may involve various issues such as contracts, property rights, employment rights, or matters related to accidents.

Criminal Courts

The court systems across England and Wales, Scotland, and Northern Ireland exhibit distinct characteristics.

Magistrates' and Justice of the Peace Courts: In England, Wales, and Northern Ireland, minor criminal cases are typically addressed in Magistrates' Courts. In Scotland, similar cases are heard in Justice of the Peace Courts. Magistrates and Justices of the Peace (JPs) are community members who usually serve voluntarily and do not require legal qualifications. They receive role-specific training and are supported by a legal adviser. In England, Wales, and Scotland, magistrates decide on the verdict and sentencing if the defendant is found guilty. In Northern Ireland, cases are adjudicated by a legally qualified District Judge or Deputy District Judge.

Crown Courts and Sheriff Courts: Serious offences in England, Wales, and Northern Ireland are tried in Crown Courts before a judge and jury. In Scotland, serious cases are heard in Sheriff Courts by a sheriff or a sheriff and jury. The most severe cases in Scotland, such as murder, are tried in the High Court with a judge and jury. Juries are composed of randomly selected members from the electoral register. In England, Wales, and Northern Ireland, juries consist of 12 members, while in Scotland, they have 15 members. Those summoned for jury duty are generally required to serve unless they are ineligible or have a valid exemption. The jury reviews the evidence and delivers a verdict of "guilty" or "not guilty," with Scotland also offering a "not proven" verdict. If found guilty, the judge determines the appropriate sentence.

Youth Courts: In England, Wales, and Northern Ireland, cases involving individuals aged 10 to 17 are usually heard in Youth Courts by up to three specially trained magistrates or a District Judge. Serious cases may be referred to the Crown Court. The accused's parents or guardians are typically expected to attend, and Youth Courts are closed to the public, with restrictions on publishing the young person's identity or photographs. In Scotland, offences committed by children and young people are addressed through the Children's Hearings System. In Northern Ireland, a youth conferencing system is used to decide appropriate measures for handling young offenders.

Civil Courts

County Courts manage a wide range of civil disputes, including debt recovery, personal injury claims, family issues, contract breaches, and divorce cases. In Scotland, many of these cases are addressed by the Sheriff Court, while more complex civil matters, such as those involving large compensation claims, are heard in the High Court in England, Wales, and Northern Ireland, or in the Court of Session in Edinburgh, Scotland.

The small claims procedure provides a straightforward and cost-effective way to resolve minor disputes, avoiding the extensive time and expense of hiring a lawyer. This procedure is applicable for claims under £5,000 in England and Wales, and under £3,000 in Scotland and Northern Ireland. The hearings are conducted in a simple setting where a judge oversees the proceedings and both parties are seated around a table. Small claims can also be filed online through the Money Claims Online platform at www.moneyclaim.gov.uk.

For more information on the small claims process, individuals should contact their local County Court or Sheriff Court. Additional details can be found through the following websites:

- **England and Wales:** www.gov.uk
- **Scotland:** www.scotcourts.gov.uk
- **Northern Ireland:** www.courtsni.gov.uk

Legal Advice

Solicitors are trained legal professionals who offer legal advice, take necessary actions on behalf of their clients, and represent them in court. They operate throughout the UK and it is important to choose a solicitor who specialises in the relevant area of law and has the appropriate experience for your case.

Solicitors often promote their services through local newspapers and directories, such as the Yellow Pages. The Citizens Advice Bureau (www.citizensadvice.org.uk) can help you find a list of local solicitors and their specialisations. Further details about solicitors and their areas of expertise are available from the Law Society (www.lawsociety.org.uk) in England and Wales, the Law Society of Scotland (www.lawscot.org.uk), or the Law Society of Northern Ireland (www.lawsoc-ni.org).

Solicitors generally charge fees based on the time spent on a case, so it's important to clarify the expected costs at the beginning.

Fundamental Principles

Throughout its history, Britain has been dedicated to protecting individual rights and preserving essential freedoms. These rights have their roots in foundational documents such as the Magna Carta, the Habeas Corpus Act, and the Bill of Rights of 1689. Over time, these rights have evolved and expanded. British diplomats and legal experts were instrumental in the creation of the European Convention on Human Rights, contributing to its drafting. In 1950, the UK was one of the first countries to sign the Convention.

The European Convention on Human Rights includes several key principles, such as:

- The right to life

- The prohibition of torture
- The prohibition of slavery and forced labour
- The right to liberty and security
- The right to a fair trial
- Freedom of thought, conscience, and religion
- Freedom of expression, including freedom of speech

To integrate the European Convention on Human Rights into UK law, the Human Rights Act of 1998 was passed. This Act requires that the government, public bodies, and courts in the UK uphold the fundamental principles set out in the Convention.

Equal Opportunities

In the UK, laws are in place to prevent unfair treatment based on factors such as age, disability, sex, pregnancy and maternity, race, religion or belief, sexuality, or marital status in any area of life or work. If you experience discrimination, various resources are available to help you. The Citizens Advice Bureau offers valuable guidance, and you can also contact the following organisations for assistance:

- **England and Wales:** Equality and Human Rights Commission (www.equalityhumanrights.com)
- **Scotland:** Equality and Human Rights Commission in Scotland (www.equalityhumanrights.com/scotland/the-commission-in-scotland) and Scottish Human Rights Commission (www.scottishhumanrights.com)
- **Northern Ireland:** Equality Commission for Northern Ireland (www.equalityni.org) and Northern Ireland Human Rights Commission (www.nihrc.org)

These organisations provide specific information and support tailored to your location within the UK.

Domestic Violence

In the UK, domestic violence, which refers to abuse and violence within the home, is a serious criminal offence. It is important to understand that anyone, irrespective of gender, marital status, or living arrangements, who perpetrates violent behavior against their partner can be prosecuted. Additionally, forcing someone, including a spouse, into sexual activity can result in a rape charge.

If you are experiencing domestic violence, it is crucial to seek help immediately. Consulting a solicitor or contacting the Citizens Advice Bureau can offer information on available options and support. In some areas, refuges or shelters provide temporary safe accommodation. For emergency assistance, helpline numbers are listed in the front section of the Yellow Pages. Women can also reach out to the nearest women's center for support. The 24-hour National Domestic Violence Freephone Helpline at 0808 2000 247 is available at all times, and the police can also help you find a safe place to stay.

Female Genital Mutilation

In the UK, female genital mutilation (FGM), also known as cutting or female circumcision, is strictly illegal. Both performing FGM and facilitating it—such as by arranging for a girl or woman to undergo the procedure abroad—are criminal offences.

Forced Marriage

In the UK, it is essential that both individuals enter a marriage willingly and freely. Arranged marriages, where both parties consent, are legally acceptable. However, forced marriage occurs when one or both individuals are coerced or unable to provide genuine consent. Forcing someone into marriage is a criminal offence.

To combat this issue, Forced Marriage Protection Orders were established in 2008 under the Forced Marriage (Civil Protection) Act 2007, applicable to England, Wales, and Northern Ireland. These court orders are designed to protect individuals from being coerced into marriage or to safeguard those already in a forced marriage. In Scotland, similar Protection Orders were introduced in November 2011.

A person who may be a victim, or someone acting on their behalf, can apply for these orders. Violating the terms of such an order can result in contempt of court charges and imprisonment for up to two years.

Revision Questions

Q1. What is required for a marriage to be considered valid in the UK?
A) Both individuals must be related
B) Both individuals must consent willingly and freely
C) Only one individual must consent
D) The marriage must be arranged by a legal advisor

Q2. What is the legal status of arranged marriages in the UK?
A) Accepted if both parties consent
B) Illegal unless performed by a religious leader
C) Only allowed with government approval
D) Prohibited unless arranged by a court

Q3. Which UK region introduced Protection Orders similar to those introduced in England, Wales, and Northern Ireland in November 2011?
A) Wales
B) Northern Ireland
C) Scotland
D) Ireland

Q4. True or false? In the UK, female genital mutilation is strictly illegal.

Answers

Q1. What is required for a marriage to be considered valid in the UK?
Answer: B – Both individuals must consent willingly and freely

Q2. What is the legal status of arranged marriages in the UK?
Answer: A – Accepted if both parties consent

Q3. Which UK region introduced Protection Orders similar to those introduced in England, Wales, and Northern Ireland in November 2011?
Answer: C – Scotland

Q4. True or false? In the UK, female genital mutilation is strictly illegal.
Answer: True

Tax, Insurance & Driving

Income Tax

In the UK, individuals are required to pay taxes on their income from various sources, including:

- Wages from employment
- Profits from self-employment
- Taxable benefits
- Pension income
- Earnings from property, savings, and dividends

The revenue from income tax supports essential government services such as infrastructure, education, policing, and the armed forces.

For most people, income tax is automatically deducted from their wages through the Pay As You Earn (PAYE) system, with payments sent directly to HM Revenue & Customs (HMRC). If you are self-employed, you must handle your own taxes through "self-assessment," which involves filling out a tax return. Additionally, certain individuals may be required to complete a tax return if HMRC sends one to them. It is important to complete and return this form promptly once you have gathered all necessary information.

For more details about income tax, visit www.hmrc.gov.uk/incometax. For assistance with taxes and tax forms, contact the HMRC self-assessment helpline at 0845 300 0627 or visit the HMRC website at www.hmrc.gov.uk.

National Insurance

In the UK, nearly everyone engaged in paid work, including those who are self-employed, must make National Insurance Contributions. These contributions fund various state benefits and services, such as the state retirement pension and the National Health Service (NHS).

For employees, National Insurance Contributions are automatically deducted from their wages by their employers. Self-employed individuals are responsible for paying their own contributions. Failure to make sufficient contributions can lead to ineligibility for certain benefits, like Jobseeker's Allowance or a full state pension. Additionally, workers with lower earnings, such as part-time employees, may not qualify for statutory payments like maternity pay if their earnings are below a specific threshold.

Detailed information on National Insurance Contributions is available on the HM Revenue & Customs (HMRC) website at www.hmrc.gov.uk/ni.

Obtaining a National Insurance Number: A National Insurance number is a unique identifier that ensures your contributions and tax payments are recorded accurately. In the UK, young people receive their National Insurance number just before their 16th birthday.

Non-UK nationals who are looking for work, starting a job, or becoming self-employed in the UK will need a National Insurance number. You can start working without one, but you must apply for it if you have permission to work in the UK. Contact the Department for Work and Pensions (DWP) to arrange obtaining a National Insurance number, and you may need to attend an interview. The DWP will guide you through the process and inform you of the required documents. Note that a National Insurance number does not prove your right to work in the UK.

For more information on applying for a National Insurance number, visit www.gov.uk.

Driving

In the UK, vehicles must always be driven on the left side of the road. To legally drive a car or motorcycle on public roads, you must be at least 17 years old and hold a valid driving licence. Obtaining a UK driving licence requires passing both a theoretical test and a practical driving assessment. For riding a moped, the minimum age is 16, and there are additional age restrictions and tests for driving larger vehicles.

Drivers can use their licence until they turn 70, at which point it must be renewed every three years.

In Northern Ireland, new drivers must display an R plate (indicating restricted driver status) for one year after passing their driving test.

If you hold a driving licence from an EU country, Iceland, Liechtenstein, or Norway, you can drive in the UK as long as your licence remains valid. For licences from other countries, you can use them in the UK for up to 12 months; after this period, you must obtain a UK full driving licence to continue driving.

All vehicles in the UK must be registered with the Driver and Vehicle Licensing Agency (DVLA). Drivers must also pay an annual road tax. Motor insurance is compulsory, and driving without it is a serious offence. Vehicles older than three years must undergo an annual Ministry of Transport (MOT) test. Failing to have a valid MOT certificate for such vehicles is an offence. For more details on vehicle tax and MOT requirements, visit www.gov.uk.

Revision Questions

Q1. What side of the road should you drive on in the UK?
A) Right
B) Left
C) Center
D) Either side

Q2. What is the minimum age required to drive a car or motorcycle on public roads in the UK?
A) 17
B) 16
C) 18
D) 21

Q3. At what age must a UK driving licence be renewed every three years?
A) 65
B) 80
C) 75
D) 70

Q4. How long can you use a driving licence from an EU country in the UK?
A) 3 months
B) 6 months
C) 12 months
D) Indefinitely

Q5. What must vehicles over three years old undergo annually in the UK?
A) A road safety inspection
B) An emissions test
C) A Ministry of Transport (MOT) test
D) A registration renewal

Q6. What must be obtained if you are self-employed in the UK?
A) A business driving permit
B) A National Insurance number
C) A special driving licence
D) A professional driving badge

Q7. True or false? The revenue from income tax supports essential government services such as infrastructure, education, policing, and the armed forces.

Q8. What is the purpose of a National Insurance number?

A) To prove your right to work in the UK

B) To register for a driving license

C) To track your national insurance contributions and tax payments

D) To obtain a passport

Answers

Q1. What side of the road should you drive on in the UK?
Answer: B – Left

Q2. What is the minimum age required to drive a car or motorcycle on public roads in the UK?
Answer: A – 17

Q3. At what age must a UK driving licence be renewed every three years?
Answer: D – 70

Q4. How long can you use a driving licence from an EU country in the UK?
Answer: D – Indefinitely
Note: EU driving licences are valid in the UK as long as they remain valid.

Q5. What must vehicles over three years old undergo annually in the UK?
Answer: C – A Ministry of Transport (MOT) test

Q6. What must be obtained if you are self-employed in the UK?
Answer: B – A National Insurance number
Note: Self-employed individuals need a National Insurance number for tax and National Insurance contributions.

Q7. True or false? The revenue from income tax supports essential government services such as infrastructure, education, policing, and the armed forces.
Answer: True

Q8. What is the purpose of a National Insurance number?
Answer: C – To track your national insurance contributions and tax payments

Your Role in the Community

Obtaining British citizenship or settling in the UK brings with it both responsibilities and opportunities. It offers individuals the chance to become actively involved in their community. This section outlines the key responsibilities of citizenship and provides guidance on how you can contribute to improving the quality of life and work within your community.

Values & Responsibilities

Although Britain is one of the most diverse societies globally, it is united by a common set of values and responsibilities that resonate with everyone. These core principles and duties include:

1. Following and respecting the law
2. Acknowledging and upholding the rights of others
3. Treating people with fairness and impartiality
4. Acting responsibly in all areas of life
5. Supporting and protecting your family
6. Respecting and caring for the environment
7. Ensuring equality for all individuals, regardless of sex, race, religion, age, disability, class, or sexual orientation
8. Working hard to support yourself and your family
9. Helping those in need
10. Engaging in local and national elections by exercising your right to vote

Adhering to these values will help you become an active and responsible citizen, contributing to a stronger and more inclusive community.

Being a Good Neighbour

When moving to a new house or apartment, it's advisable to introduce yourself to your new neighbours. Building relationships with those living nearby helps you integrate into the community and make new friends. Neighbours can also be valuable resources, such as caring for your pets while you are away or providing advice on local services and amenities.

Being considerate of your neighbours' privacy and managing noise levels can help avoid conflicts. Additionally, keeping your garden well-maintained and ensuring that refuse bags and bins are placed in the proper locations only on collection days helps maintain a pleasant neighbourhood environment. By being mindful of these practices, you foster positive interactions and contribute to a harmonious living experience for everyone in the community.

Getting Involved in Local Activities

Volunteering and actively supporting your community are crucial aspects of being a responsible and engaged citizen. These activities help you integrate into the community, build relationships, and contribute to its improvement. When people assist one another, it has a positive effect on the overall quality of life in the area. Moreover, volunteering allows you to uphold your responsibilities as a citizen by encouraging responsible behaviour and providing help to those in need. Through your active involvement, you help create a stronger, more supportive, and united community.

How You Can Support Your Community

There are many positive ways to contribute to your community and show good citizenship.

Jury Service

In addition to the right to vote, individuals listed on the electoral roll may be randomly selected to serve on a jury. Anyone aged 18 to 70 who is registered can be chosen for this duty.

Helping in Schools

Parents can actively support their children's schools in several ways, such as helping in classrooms, assisting with various school activities, or supporting reading programs. Schools often organise fundraising events like book sales, toy sales, or food stalls to raise additional funds. You might also come up with your own fundraising ideas. Parent-teacher associations (PTAs) often manage these events. Volunteering or joining the PTA benefits the school and helps you connect with your local community. Check school notices or communications from your children for these opportunities.

School Governors

School governors, or members of the school board in Scotland, are community members dedicated to improving children's education. There is no upper age limit, but candidates must be at least 18 years old. Governors have three main responsibilities:

1. Setting the strategic direction for the school.
2. Ensuring the school is held accountable.
3. Monitoring and evaluating the school's performance. To find out about governor or school board openings, contact your local school or apply online through the School Governors' One-Stop Shop at www.sgoss.org.uk. In England, there's also an opportunity for parents and community groups to apply to establish a free school in their area. More details are available on the Department for Education website at www.dfe.gov.uk.

Supporting Political Parties

Political parties welcome new members who wish to support specific viewpoints and engage in the democratic process. During elections, parties become very active, with members working to persuade voters through activities such as distributing leaflets or canvassing door-to-door. You are not required to share your voting intentions with canvassers if you prefer not to. British citizens can run for various positions, including local councillor, Member of Parliament, or Member of the European Parliament. Irish citizens, eligible Commonwealth citizens, or EU nationals (except for standing as an MP) may also be eligible for some positions. For more information on joining a political party, visit the respective party websites.

Helping With Local Services

Numerous volunteering opportunities exist with local services, such as hospitals, youth projects, universities, housing associations, museums, and arts councils. These organisations seek community involvement in their operations. If you're interested in law enforcement, consider roles like special constable, lay representative (a non-police role), or magistrate. Vacancies are often listed in local newspapers or on local radio stations. Additional details about these roles can be found at www.gov.uk. Volunteering in these capacities allows you to make a significant impact in your local community.

Blood & Organ Donation

Donating blood is essential for hospitals to treat a wide array of injuries and illnesses. The blood donation process usually takes around an hour. If you are interested in donating blood, you can sign up at the following websites:

- England and North Wales: www.blood.co.uk
- Rest of Wales: www.welsh-blood.org.uk
- Scotland: www.scotblood.co.uk
- Northern Ireland: www.nibts.org

Organ donation also offers a valuable way to make a difference. By registering as an organ donor, you help ease the decision-making process for your family regarding organ donation after your death. You can register to be an organ donor at www.organdonation.nhs.uk. Additionally, you can choose to donate a kidney while alive.

Volunteering provides a fulfilling way to support various causes and positively impact your community. It offers benefits such as meeting new people, developing skills, and enhancing your CV. Volunteer activities can help you practice English, gain work-related skills, or simply fulfill a desire to help others.

There are many volunteering opportunities available, including:

- Working with animals, like at a local rescue shelter
- Engaging in youth work, such as volunteering at a youth group
- Participating in environmental improvement, such as local litter clean-up events
- Assisting the homeless, for example, at a homeless shelter
- Providing mentoring support to individuals recently released from prison
- Contributing to health and hospitals, such as working at a hospital information desk
- Helping older people, such as volunteering at a residential care home

The UK hosts a diverse array of charities and voluntary organisations focused on improving lives, supporting animals, and protecting the environment. These include large international organisations like the British Red Cross and smaller local charities. Examples include:

- Age UK (for older people)
- NSPCC (for children)

- Crisis and Shelter (for the homeless)
- Cancer Research UK (for medical research)
- National Trust and Friends of the Earth (for environmental protection)
- PDSA (for animal welfare)

Volunteers are vital for these organisations and their fundraising efforts. Opportunities are often listed in local newspapers and on charity websites. For more information about volunteering, visit www.do-it.org.uk.

Young people also have numerous volunteering options, some offering accreditation to aid skill development. Programs like the National Citizen Service offer 16- and 17-year-olds outdoor activities, skill development, and community projects. For more details, check:

- National Citizen Service: nationalcitizenservice.direct.gov.uk
- England: www.vinspired.com
- Wales: www.gwirvol.org
- Scotland: www.vds.org.uk
- Northern Ireland: www.volunteernow.co.uk

Looking After the Environment

Maximizing recycling efforts and minimizing waste is essential for environmental sustainability. Using recycled materials in manufacturing conserves energy and reduces the need for new raw materials. Additionally, recycling helps decrease the volume of waste sent to landfills.

For detailed information about recycling and its benefits, visit www.recyclenow.com. This site offers guidance on what can be recycled at home and in your local area if you live in England. For Wales, visit www.wasteawarenesswales.org.uk; for Scotland, go to www.recycleforscotland.com; and for Northern Ireland, consult your local authority.

Supporting your local community by buying products locally is another way to make a positive impact. This practice benefits local businesses and farmers, supports the British economy, and reduces your carbon footprint, as local products have shorter transportation distances compared to imports.

Choosing to walk or use public transportation whenever possible further benefits the environment by reducing pollution from personal vehicles. This simple choice helps protect the environment and contributes to a cleaner, greener community.

Revision Questions

Q1. True or false? Anyone living in the UK can be selected for jury duty.

Q2. What does the term "volunteering" refer to?
A) Working without pay to support a cause
B) Taking paid work to support a cause
C) Mandatorily participating in community projects
D) Running a business for profit

Q3. What is a key benefit of choosing public transportation over personal vehicles?
A) Increased pollution
B) Higher transportation costs
C) Reduced pollution
D) Longer travel times

Answers

Q1. True or false? Anyone living in the UK can be selected for jury duty.

Answer: False – Jury duty is limited to citizens aged 18 to 70.

Q2. What does the term "volunteering" refer to?

Answer: A – Working without pay to support a cause

Q3. What is a key benefit of choosing public transportation over personal vehicles?

Answer: C – Reduced pollution

Note: Public transportation reduces the pollution generated by personal vehicles.

Chapter 6: Practice Tests

In this chapter, you will find a range of questions covering various topics, including history, government, legal systems, and daily life in the UK. You may like to write down your answers on a piece of paper or answer them in your head.

After each question, you will have the opportunity to check your answer. By working through these questions, you'll also gain confidence and improve your ability to recall important information under timed conditions.

However, feel free to pause, revisit sections of the book, or take additional notes as needed. The more you practice, the more prepared you will be for the actual test. Remember, the goal is not just to answer questions correctly but to deepen your grasp of British history, culture, government, and societal norms.

We wish you the best of luck on your journey to becoming a UK citizen.

Now, get ready for the practice tests!

Practice Test 1

Q1. What is the capital city of the UK?
A) London
B) Edinburgh
C) Cardiff
D) Belfast

Q2. Who is the current monarch of the United Kingdom as of 2025?
A) Queen Elizabeth II
B) King Charles III
C) Prince William
D) Queen Anne

Q3. Which document established the principle that everyone is subject to the law, even the monarch?
A) The Magna Carta
B) The Bill of Rights
C) The Habeas Corpus Act
D) The European Convention on Human Rights

Q4. What is the minimum age required to vote in UK general elections?
A) 16
B) 18
C) 21
D) 25

Q5. Which of the following is NOT a devolved nation within the UK?
A) Scotland
B) Wales
C) Northern Ireland
D) Gibraltar

Q6. What is the role of the House of Lords in the UK Parliament?
A) To create laws
B) To represent the public
C) To review and revise legislation
D) To manage local government

Q7. Who is responsible for collecting taxes in the UK?
A) The Treasury
B) HM Revenue & Customs (HMRC)
C) The Bank of England
D) The Department for Work and Pensions

Q8. Which of the following is a key principle of the European Convention on Human Rights?

A) Right to bear arms
B) Right to a fair trial
C) Right to private property
D) Right to free education

Q9. When does the UK's financial year typically start?

A) January 1
B) April 1
C) July 1
D) October 1

Q10. What is the purpose of the National Insurance contributions in the UK?

A) To fund public transport
B) To support educational institutions
C) To pay for military expenses
D) To finance state benefits and services

Q11. Which of the following is a requirement to apply for a UK driving licence?

A) You must be at least 16 years old
B) You must pass a driving test
C) You must own a car
D) You must be a UK citizen

Q12. What is the main purpose of recycling?

A) To reduce waste and conserve energy
B) To increase the cost of goods
C) To create new waste products
D) To promote international trade

Q13. What is the primary role of the UK's local councils?

A) To create national legislation
B) To manage local services and facilities
C) To oversee international relations
D) To regulate national businesses

Q14. What age must you be to legally drink alcohol in a public place in the UK?

A) 16
B) 18
C) 21
D) 25

Q15. Which of the following is a key responsibility of British citizens?

A) To avoid paying taxes
B) To follow the law
C) To refuse jury service
D) To ignore local government rules

Q16. What is a Forced Marriage Protection Order designed to do?

A) Prevent domestic violence
B) Stop individuals from entering the UK
C) Protect people from being forced into marriage
D) Restrict international travel

Q17. Which of the following is NOT a typical role of a school governor?

A) Setting the strategic direction of the school
B) Ensuring accountability within the school
C) Teaching individual subjects
D) Monitoring and evaluating school performance

Q18. How often must UK citizens renew their driving licence after age 70?

A) Every year
B) Every 2 years
C) Every 3 years
D) Every 5 years

Q19. What is the main aim of the NHS?

A) To provide education
B) To offer free healthcare services
C) To regulate business
D) To manage local transportation

Q20. Which English king was forced to sign the Magna Carta in 1215?

A) Henry III
B) Richard the Lionheart
C) Elizabeth
D) John

Q21. What is the primary function of the UK Parliament?

A) To enforce laws
B) To make and debate laws
C) To manage public services
D) To provide financial aid

Q22. Which British Prime Minister became famous for his speeches during the Second World War?

A) Neville Chamberlain

B) Stanley Baldwin

C) Winston Churchill

D) Clement Attlee

Q23. Where is the Parliament that governs the United Kingdom located?

A) Westminster

B) Cardiff

C) Belfast

D) Edinburgh

Q24. How often do vehicles over three years old need an MOT test?

A) Every 6 months

B) Annually

C) Every 2 years

D) Every 5 years

Answers

Q1. What is the capital city of the UK?
Answer: A – London

Q2. Who is the current monarch of the United Kingdom as of 2025?
Answer: B – King Charles III

Q3. Which document established the principle that everyone is subject to the law, even the monarch?
Answer: A – The Magna Carta

Q4. What is the minimum age required to vote in UK general elections?
Answer: B – 18

Q5. Which of the following is NOT a devolved nation within the UK?
Answer: D – Gibraltar

Q6. What is the role of the House of Lords in the UK Parliament?
Answer: C – To review and revise legislation

Q7. Who is responsible for collecting taxes in the UK?
Answer: B – HM Revenue & Customs (HMRC)

Q8. Which of the following is a key principle of the European Convention on Human Rights?
Answer: B – Right to a fair trial

Q9. When does the UK's financial year typically start?
Answer: B – April 1

Q10. What is the purpose of the National Insurance contributions in the UK?
Answer: D – To finance state benefits and services

Q11. Which of the following is a requirement to apply for a UK driving licence?
Answer: B – You must pass a driving test

Q12. What is the main purpose of recycling?
Answer: A – To reduce waste and conserve energy

Q13. What is the primary role of the UK's local councils?

Answer: B – To manage local services and facilities

Q14. What age must you be to legally drink alcohol in a public place in the UK?

Answer: B – 18

Q15. Which of the following is a key responsibility of British citizens?

Answer: B – To follow the law

Q16. What is a Forced Marriage Protection Order designed to do?

Answer: C – Protect people from being forced into marriage

Q17. Which of the following is NOT a typical role of a school governor?

Answer: C – Teaching individual subjects

Q18. How often must UK citizens renew their driving licence after age 70?

Answer: C – Every 3 years

Q19. What is the main aim of the NHS?

Answer: B – To offer free healthcare services

Q20. Which English king was forced to sign the Magna Carta in 1215?

Answer: D – John

Q21. What is the primary function of the UK Parliament?

Answer: B – To make and debate laws

Q22. Which British Prime Minister became famous for his speeches during the Second World War?

Answer: C – Winston Churchill

Q23. Where is the Parliament that governs the United Kingdom located?

Answer: A – Westminster

Q24. How often do vehicles over three years old need an MOT test?

Answer: B – Annually

Practice Test 2

Q1. Who were the first inhabitants of Britain during the Stone Age?

A) Hunter-gatherers
B) Anglo-Saxons
C) Vikings
D) Pirates

Q2. Which of the following is the national flower of Wales?

A) Rose
B) Thistle
C) Daffodil
D) Shamrock

Q3. What is the role of the Prime Minister in the UK?

A) To interpret laws
B) To manage international relations
C) To lead the government
D) To oversee local councils

Q4. Which event does the UK celebrate on November 5th?

A) Remembrance Day
B) Bonfire Night
C) Christmas Day
D) St. George's Day

Q5. Which UK city is famous for its university and the annual Oxford-Cambridge boat race?

A) Cambridge
B) London
C) Oxford
D) Edinburgh

Q6. What is the purpose of a General Election in the UK?

A) To appoint local mayors
B) To elect Members of Parliament
C) To approve local council budgets
D) To review police performance

Q7. Which of the following is a British Overseas Territory?

A) Gibraltar
B) Bermuda
C) Cyprus
D) Malta

Q8. Which monarch celebrated their Diamond Jubilee in 2012?

A) Elizabeth I
B) Elizabeth II
C) Elizabeth III
D) Victoria

Q9. Which UK law protects people from discrimination in the workplace?

A) The Equality Act 2010
B) The Employment Rights Act 1996
C) The Human Rights Act 1998
D) The Health and Safety at Work Act 1974

Q10. What is the significance of the Union Jack?

A) It is the flag of Scotland.
B) It is the national flag of the UK.
C) It represents the European Union.
D) It is the flag of England.

Q11. What age must you be to legally drive a car in the UK?

A) 16
B) 17
C) 18
D) 21

Q12. Which of the following is a major British festival celebrated in August?

A) The Edinburgh Festival Fringe
B) St. Patrick's Day
C) Halloween
D) Christmas

Q13. Who is the head of the Church of England?

A) The Archbishop of Canterbury
B) The Prime Minister
C) The monarch
D) The Pope

Q14. Which of the following countries is not part of the United Kingdom?

A) England
B) Scotland
C) Republic of Ireland
D) Wales

Q15. Which UK city is known for its historic Roman baths?

A) Bath
B) London

C) York

D) Canterbury

Q16. What is the role of the House of Commons in the UK Parliament?

A) To review laws

B) To draft and pass legislation

C) To oversee local councils

D) To appoint judges

Q17. Which of the following is a responsibility of the UK's local government?

A) Setting national tax rates

B) Managing national defense

C) Running local schools and services

D) Negotiating international treaties

Q18. What is the minimum age for alcohol consumption in private settings in the UK?

A) 16

B) 17

C) 18

D) 21

Q19. Which historic document limited the power of the monarch and established the principle of due process?

A) The Bill of Rights

B) The Magna Carta

C) The Habeas Corpus Act

D) The Act of Settlement

Q20. Which public service is funded through National Insurance contributions?

A) Education

B) Public transportation

C) Healthcare

D) Housing

Q21. Which major tennis tournament is held annually at the All England Lawn Tennis and Croquet Club?

A) The US Open

B) The French Open

C) The Ashes

D) Wimbledon

Q22. True or false? Oliver Cromwell was a member of the royal family.

Q23. What is the address of the House of Commons?
A) The Tower of London
B) The Palace of Westminster, London
C) The House of Lords, Westminster
D) 10 Downing Street, London

Q24. Which famous British author wrote the Harry Potter series?
A) J.R.R. Tolkien
B) Agatha Christie
C) J.K. Rowling
D) C.S. Lewis

Answers

Q1. Who were the first inhabitants of Britain during the Stone Age?
Answer: A – Hunter-gatherers

Q2. Which of the following is the national flower of Wales?
Answer: C – Daffodil

Q3. What is the role of the Prime Minister in the UK?
Answer: C – To lead the government

Q4. Which event does the UK celebrate on November 5th?
Answer: B – Bonfire Night

Q5. Which UK city is famous for its university and the annual Oxford-Cambridge boat race?
Answer: C – Oxford

Q6. What is the purpose of a General Election in the UK?
Answer: B – To elect Members of Parliament

Q7. Which of the following is a British Overseas Territory?
Answer: A – Gibraltar

Q8. Which monarch celebrated their Diamond Jubilee in 2012?
Answer: B – Elizabeth II

Q9. Which UK law protects people from discrimination in the workplace?
Answer: A – The Equality Act 2010

Q10. What is the significance of the Union Jack?
Answer: B – It is the national flag of the UK.

Q11. What age must you be to legally drive a car in the UK?
Answer: B – 17

Q12. Which of the following is a major British festival celebrated in August?
Answer: A – The Edinburgh Festival Fringe

Q13. Who is the head of the Church of England?
Answer: C – The monarch

Q14. Which of the following countries is not part of the United Kingdom?

Answer: C – Republic of Ireland

Q15. Which UK city is known for its historic Roman baths?
Answer: A – Bath

Q16. What is the role of the House of Commons in the UK Parliament?
Answer: B – To draft and pass legislation

Q17. Which of the following is a responsibility of the UK's local government?
Answer: C – Running local schools and services

Q18. What is the minimum age for alcohol consumption in private settings in the UK?
Answer: C – 18

Q19. Which historic document limited the power of the monarch and established the principle of due process?
Answer: B – The Magna Carta

Q20. Which public service is funded through National Insurance contributions?
Answer: C – Healthcare

Q21. Which major tennis tournament is held annually at the All England Lawn Tennis and Croquet Club?
Answer: D – Wimbledon

Q22. True or false? Oliver Cromwell was a member of the royal family.
Answer: False

Q23. What is the address of the House of Commons?
Answer: B – The Palace of Westminster, London

Q24. Which famous British author wrote the Harry Potter series?
Answer: C – J.K. Rowling

Practice Test 3

Q1. Which of the following is a traditional British dish made of minced meat and mashed potatoes?

A) Shepherd's Pie
B) Roast Beef
C) Bangers and Mash
D) Cornish Pasty

Q2. What is the official residence of the Prime Minister of the UK?

A) Buckingham Palace
B) 10 Downing Street
C) The Palace of Westminster
D) Windsor Castle

Q3. What is the name of the UK's national anthem?

A) God Save the King
B) Rule Britannia
C) Land of Hope and Glory
D) Jerusalem

Q4. Which UK city is known for the famous Stonehenge monument?

A) Bath
B) Salisbury
C) Exeter
D) Bristol

Q5. Which famous British scientist developed the theory of evolution?

A) Isaac Newton
B) Charles Darwin
C) Albert Einstein
D) Michael Faraday

Q6. What is the official currency of the United Kingdom?

A) The Dollar
B) The British Coin
C) The Euro
D) The Pound Sterling

Q7. What is the name of the UK's highest mountain?

A) Snowdon
B) Scafell Pike
C) Ben Nevis
D) Helvellyn

Q8. What is commonly eaten on Shrove Tuesday in the UK?

A) Breakfast in bed
B) Pancakes
C) French fries
D) Pudding

Q9. Which historical event took place in 1066?

A) The English Civil War
B) The Battle of Hastings
C) The signing of the Magna Carta
D) The Battle of Waterloo

Q10. Which British author is famous for the "James Bond" series?

A) Ian Fleming
B) Agatha Christie
C) J.K. Rowling
D) John le Carré

Q11. Who was the longest-standing Prime Minister of the 20th Century?

A) Winston Churchill
B) Tony Blair
C) Boris Johnson
D) Margaret Thatcher

Q12. Which English king is famous for marrying six wives?

A) Henry II
B) Charles III
C) Henry VIII
D) Henry VI

Q13. Which is not a play written by William Shakespeare>

A) Hamlet
B) Macbeth
C) Romeo and Juliet
D) Braveheart

Q14. What is the minimum age requirement to stand for election as a Member of Parliament (MP) in the UK?

A) 16
B) 18
C) 21
D) 25

Q15. Which British prime minister introduced the National Health Service (NHS)?

A) Winston Churchill
B) Clement Attlee
C) Margaret Thatcher
D) Tony Blair

Q16. Which type of court in the UK deals with serious criminal cases?

A) Magistrates' Court
B) Crown Court
C) County Court
D) High Court

Q17. What is the name of the UK's oldest university?

A) University of Cambridge
B) University of Oxford
C) University of Edinburgh
D) University of London

Q18. Who opened the first Indian restaurant in Britain?

A) Rudyard Kipling
B) Mohammed Iqbal
C) Rishi Sunak
D) Sake Dean Mahomet

Q19. In which city is the British Museum located?

A) Manchester
B) London
C) Birmingham
D) Leeds

Q20. Which British landmark is known for its large stone monoliths arranged in a circular pattern?

A) Stonehenge
B) Hadrian's Wall
C) The Tower of London
D) The Giant's Causeway

Q21. Which British monarch was known for her long reign and significant influence over the British Empire during the 19th century?

A) Queen Elizabeth I
B) Queen Victoria
C) Queen Elizabeth II
D) Queen Anne

Q22. What is the name of the British award given annually for the best novel written in English?

A) The Booker Prize
B) The Pulitzer Prize
C) The Nobel Prize in Literature
D) The Whitbread Award

Q23. What does the term "Borough" refer to in the UK?

A) A type of local government district
B) A large rural estate
C) A historical castle
D) A type of educational institution

Q24. Which British author wrote "The Chronicles of Narnia" series?

A) Philip Pullman
B) J.R.R. Tolkien
C) Roald Dahl
D) C.S. Lewis

Answers

Q1. Which of the following is a traditional British dish made of minced meat and mashed potatoes?
Answer: A – Shepherd's Pie

Q2. What is the official residence of the Prime Minister of the UK?
Answer: B – 10 Downing Street

Q3. What is the name of the UK's national anthem?
Answer: A – God Save the King

Q4. Which UK city is known for the famous Stonehenge monument?
Answer: B – Salisbury

Q5. Which famous British scientist developed the theory of evolution?
Answer: B – Charles Darwin

Q6. What is the official currency of the United Kingdom?
Answer: D – The Pound Sterling

Q7. What is the name of the UK's highest mountain?
Answer: C – Ben Nevis

Q8. What is commonly eaten on Shrove Tuesday in the UK?
Answer: B – Pancakes

Q9. Which historical event took place in 1066?
Answer: B – The Battle of Hastings

Q10. Which British author is famous for the "James Bond" series?
Answer: A – Ian Fleming

Q11. Who was the longest-standing Prime Minister of the 20th Century?
Answer: D – Margaret Thatcher

Q12. Which English king is famous for marrying six wives?
Answer: C – Henry VIII

Q13. Which is not a play written by William Shakespeare>
Answer: D – Braveheart

Q14. What is the minimum age requirement to stand for election as a Member of Parliament (MP) in the UK?

Answer: B – 18

Q15. Which British prime minister introduced the National Health Service (NHS)?
Answer: B – Clement Attlee

Q16. Which type of court in the UK deals with serious criminal cases?
Answer: B – Crown Court

Q17. What is the name of the UK's oldest university?
Answer: B – University of Oxford

Q18. Who opened the first Indian restaurant in Britain?
Answer: D – Sake Dean Mahomet

Q19. In which city is the British Museum located?
Answer: B – London

Q20. Which British landmark is known for its large stone monoliths arranged in a circular pattern?
Answer: A – Stonehenge

Q21. Which British monarch was known for her long reign and significant influence over the British Empire during the 19th century?
Answer: B – Queen Victoria

Q22. What is the name of the British award given annually for the best novel written in English?
Answer: A – The Booker Prize

Q23. What does the term "Borough" refer to in the UK?
Answer: A – A type of local government district

Q24. Which British author wrote "The Chronicles of Narnia" series?
Answer: D – C.S. Lewis

Printed in Dunstable, United Kingdom